# KICKASS
# HUSBAND

# KICKASS
# HUSBAND

## WINNING AT LIFE, MARRIAGE & SEX

Because Happily Ever After
Doesn't Just Happen

### MATTHEW P. HOFFMAN
#### AND CHRIS CAMBAS, LMFT

**KCN**
PUBLISHING

All proceeds to support charitable causes: couples who need counseling but cannot afford it, children, education, and worthy religious institutions.

Designed by Megan Jones Design, meganjonesdesign.com

Printed in the United States of America

First Printing, 2021

ISBN 978-1-7377544-0-4

KCN Publishing
Greenville, South Carolina

# CONTENTS

**To Kimberly.**
You are at the center of my desire to be
a better husband, father, friend, and son.

# FOREWORD

THE TRUE MEASURE of any husband is what his wife has to say about him. Yesterday, my wife walked up to me in our kitchen and handed me a list titled "Ten Things I Love About You." It was basically my marriage report card. I won't bore you with the details. Let's just say that when I read it, I felt like a kickass husband.

I haven't always felt that way. In fact, for most of my adult life, I was self-centered, apathetic, and controlling. I didn't know how to shake these tendencies. They felt like part of my identity, and I thought if I let go of them, I would lose a part of who I was. Not surprisingly, I had a series of relationships that ended badly.

By my late thirties, I knew it was time to level up from bachelor to family man, but making that transition seemed impossible. I was dating the woman of my dreams, but I put off proposing to her because I secretly doubted I could be a good husband.

Everything changed the day I made a decision to be an epic husband and father. I didn't know *how* I would do it, but I was certain about what I wanted my marriage to look like. And since I made that decision and chose to live it out daily, I've been blessed with a marriage that surpassed anything I expected.

I'm here to tell you that you too can be a kickass husband. And you'll have an advantage I did not, because you'll have this book as a roadmap. Matthew Hoffman and Chris Cambas have laid out everything you need to know. Matthew generously shares stories from his own twenty-five-year marriage, and Chris contributes his perspective as a couples therapist. Together, they cover all the principles that are essential to a sound, loving relationship.

Maybe you don't feel anything like a kickass husband right now. Maybe your marriage is on the rocks. Maybe you're struggling with your demons, and the guilt and shame is tearing you up inside. Wherever you are in your marriage journey right now is okay. It doesn't matter where you start; all that matters is that you head in the right direction.

I urge you to make the decision today to become the kickass husband your wife is waiting for. You both deserve a happy marriage. With this book as your guide, you will finally experience the peace, love, and joy that are your birthright.

—JOSEPH WARREN,
Top 100 podcast host, entrepreneur,
and founder of BlowUpRocks.com

# ACKNOWLEDGMENTS

I WANT TO thank my wife, Kimberly, for inspiring me to write about how I learned to prioritize her as my number-one human relationship. It has been through her love, commitment, and support that I have discovered just how good my marriage can be and have been filled to overflowing with an unconditional love that remains long after all other fleeting joys have dissipated.

I want to thank my mother, Marcia P. Hoffman, for teaching me what it means to be a loving soul and a true man, and how to prioritize others' needs before my own.

I want to thank Chris Cambas, my co-author on this book, for his sincere friendship, his teaching, and his leadership, which have helped me keep investing in and strengthening my marriage. I am so grateful that he was up for the adventure of creating a resource for couples who want to level up their number-one relationship.

—MATTHEW P. HOFFMAN

# INTRODUCTION

IN THE TIME it takes you to read this introduction, four different couples in the United States will have gotten divorced. When you got married, did you ever think it might be the beginning of the end—a slow death of the joy, satisfaction, and fulfillment in your life? Did you honestly think things were automatically going to be honeymoon hot for the rest of your married days?

This book is full of tools, strategies, and real examples that will help you become a kickass husband and a kickass couple. You too can create a deep and abiding love—a relationship that is built to last and will shine for a lifetime.

Being a kickass husband and a kickass couple has nothing to do with being superheroes, having out-of-this-world powers, or looking like supermodels with chiseled muscles and million-dollar smiles. We all struggle with imperfections in our lives and our relationships as we try to make sense of the commitments, communication, and conflicts that arise each and every day in the relationship that should be at the top of our list.

Would you believe me if I told you that all relationships fall into one of three categories?

1. Thriving
2. Maintaining
3. Declining (or even DOA, dead on arrival)

Where are you in your marriage, your number-one relationship, right now?

After twenty years of marriage, I found myself in the dangerous no-man's-land between maintaining and declining. My wife and I had three beautiful children, a great house, close friends, and an enriching social life. We were each fully engaged in churches, our children's school, and our respective careers—a formula for what most would consider success. But we both felt there was a lot missing.

We were still committed to each other, but not in a way that was bringing out the best in one another. Arguments and disagreements were about proving who was right and breaking each other down instead of instilling unconditional love, confidence, and support. We didn't have many shared activities and interests, and our romance and intimacy were barely warm, not even at a low simmer. That's when we decided to double down and invest heavily in our number-one relationship.

By renewing our commitment, learning how to communicate more effectively, and working on resolving the conflicts that were solvable, we began to take our relationship where we both wanted it to be. We are now in that rolling boil where our married life is passionate, exciting, truly rewarding, and fulfilling.

I can honestly say that today, my relationship with my wife is better than I ever could have imagined when we first got married. The intimacy, happiness, joy, trust, and fun we have together is just incredible. We are constantly pouring into one another, investing, growing, nurturing, and encouraging each other. Through study, reading, and videos, we have learned deeper, more intimate communication. We've made a renewed, living commitment to apply the right ideas and practices in our daily lives together.

My wife and I became a kickass couple, and you and your partner can too. I and my coauthor, Chris Cambas, a licensed and actively practicing marriage therapist, have laid out fifty-two short, digestible chapters that will give you unique insight and practical ideas on how to weave the fabric of a successful, meaningful, and fulfilling relationship.

Each chapter highlights a story that showcases an idea in action and then pulls out the concepts that underpin the story's meaning and application in your relationship—and you can read these chapters in just a few short minutes each. All of the stories represent the actual events and challenges my wife and I faced, as well as what I did to strengthen my relationship. I also show you the rewards my wife and I reaped by unequivocally committing to consistently investing in our relationship. In his reflections at the end of each chapter, Chris will point out key principles and why these practices are important. These two viewpoints, taken together, will give you specific tools that can greatly improve your own relationship.

Much of our work is based on forty years of research by John Gottman. In *The Seven Principles for Making Marriage Work*,[1] Gottman uses the metaphor of a house to explain what makes some people masters of relationship. The floors of the sound relationship house are *love mapping, sharing fondness and admiration, turning toward, accepting influence, solving the solvable and creating dialogue around the perpetual, making life dreams come true*, and *creating shared meaning*. The walls of the house consist of commitment and trust. Throughout the chapters, Chris will be pointing out how these concepts come into play. See the glossary for a complete definition of each.

One word of caution: This book is not a silver bullet to kill the demons. It will not instantly put your relationship on steroids.

It is a book that tells stories that might sound a lot like your life and what you have experienced. It will teach you how and why to invest in your relationship so you too can live in that "thriving" zone. Wouldn't you like to have your relationship at that rolling boil where happiness, fun, trust, communication, intimacy, and great sex are the norm?

Think of the last time an issue arose in your relationship. Did you turn toward your spouse and lean in with love so the issue could be treated, dissolved, and put into the right perspective? Why don't you make that move today by getting close, grabbing their hand, and investing in that number-one relationship? It will pay a lifetime of dividends and fill you today with what you've been looking for all along.

# 1: WATCH THE SUNRISE

THE MOMENT I see the sun emerge from the darkened horizon, I am reminded of newness, opportunity, and promise. At sunrise, the sun appears to be climbing out of darkness and moving upon the earth—a contradiction to what we know to be true through our study of astronomy and the universe we live in. The dawning of a fresh day brings promise, renewal, and that "new birth" that seems to be free of the care, concern, and baggage that may have been weighing us down from the day before. Sunrise is also that clean, dark canvas that reveals a unique and beautiful work of art painted upon the sky. Color, shadow, and free-form shapes appear, followed by a beautiful glow and a gentle, warming light that melts away darkness and doubt.

My wife Kim and I were pregnant with our first child and in the final trimester. Delivery—our own new birth—was right around the corner, but it couldn't come soon enough! Kim was at the stage where, more than anything, she wanted that baby on the outside instead of wreaking havoc on her insides. Sleep deprivation, a steady discomfort, and back pain were just a few of the symptoms that dogged her and made me feel disconnected and helpless. I had to do something to change the pace and bring some joy into our relationship.

One night I decided we were going to get up early the next day and go watch the sunrise. I prepared a nice picnic breakfast with some fresh-baked muffins, fruit, and a thermos of coffee. I packed my boom box (remember those?) and a CD of gentle instrumental music. I woke Kim up while it was still dark and quiet. We drove to a nearby island community and parked at the water's edge facing east. I put the tailgate down on our SUV and set up our picnic. Then we sat covered in blankets, waiting for the sun to arrive. We talked about the excitement and anticipation of our long-awaited arrival. We talked about how life would change and affirmed our love and commitment to one another.

Before we were married, I had been in a full-court press, constantly looking for ways to show Kim I loved her. It had been a while since I had taken the initiative to do something special, something that would remind us of the strong bonds that tied us together. A little changeup in the routine and the quiet recognition of something beautiful and awe inspiring brought us back into gratitude mode and helped us see more of the good we were experiencing in every area of our lives.

A little effort, a little planning, and something we take for granted becomes a blessing and a loving gift to the people we treasure. What can you do to remind your partner of her incredible value to you? How can you take delight together in something like the sunrise that happens each and every day?

## CHRIS'S TAKE

In Matthew's story, we see the concepts of *trustworthiness*, *turning away*, and *turning toward*. Each of these is vital to understand if our relationships are going to thrive, particularly in such a consequential time as pregnancy. Here's why each of these concepts is important.

Matthew was feeling a little turned away from, and in response he chose to turn toward. He didn't increase the distance by turning away himself, a response that would've made a very delicate time in life even more difficult. By turning toward Kim, he opened the doors not only to a lovely day but to a day when he and his wife were able to embrace what lay ahead, and share hopes and dreams around their new family. In so doing, he increased the basis of trustworthiness in the relationship.

Trustworthiness is built on deep trust, which is a very different thing than simple trust. If you were walking through the mall and fell, you would probably hold an inherent belief that someone would help you. That's trust. It's a very small thing and something we engage in every day. Deep trust, on the other hand, can take fifteen to twenty years to fully develop.[2] It's a heartfelt sense, a sincere belief, that our spouse will be there for us when we are sick, that they will put us in front of friends, family, and career—they have our back.

Building deep trust is accomplished only through the process of turning toward, defined by John Gottman as "making an effort every day to reach out to your partner and accept their bids for emotional connection."[3] These are the small things in life. For example, you are texting and your spouse speaks to you. In that moment, you can turn toward her and engage. You can "turn away," unconsciously or willfully disengaging from your partner's bids for emotional connection, and being silent. You could even turn against her by being belligerent about the interruption. When we consistently turn toward—when that is the trend line, even though we are not perfect—we slowly and steadily build trustworthiness.

Here are a few ideas you can implement today. When your spouse speaks, engage her. Do not turn away. We know it's difficult to listen to stories that may not pique your interest, but you must. These simple acts are not only a turning toward, they are an opportunity to really get to know your wife. In taking the requisite time to do this, you'll build trustworthiness as well as the overall level of friendship you experience in the relationship.

# 2: WRITE A LETTER

WHEN WAS THE last time you received a handwritten letter from your best friend and life partner? I'll bet, like me, you have a hidden stash somewhere, a drawer filled with meaningful handwritten notes, letters, or cards that express the deep, abiding love and appreciation your better half has for you.

Letter writing is a lost art. The norm for communication today is a quick check-in by text, a recorded voice memo so you don't have to take the time to type with your thumbs, or, now, a one-character emoji meant to convey your feelings or mood with minimal effort. I admit it: I'm guilty. We're all looking for that shortcut, that make-it-easy, "real-quick" solution to communication. Since when is it a distasteful chore to use the written word to share our true feelings with someone we love and adore?

A love note can give you a warm, teary-eyed feeling beyond any emoji. Remember the excitement of going through the mail and finding a note with a familiar return address and your own name written in beloved handwriting? Would you throw all the other mail aside, tear open the note, and read it immediately? Or, like me, would you go through all the other mail, setting the letter aside until you could step away from the world and savor it in a quiet oasis with the author of those personal words? The written word has the power to transport us—to enclose us in a special moment shared only with that person writing to us.

I often work away from my home. I occasionally write letters to my wife so she'll get them when I'm not there and have the quiet, reflective opportunity to hear me speaking to her in a different, personal way. When she's frustrated with a relationship, mourning the loss of a close friend or family member, or celebrating a specific accomplishment, I take the time to share my love, respect, and commitment to her using the written word.

You can do the same for the person who matters most to you. It does not have to be an epistle or a long, drawn-out work of prose. It can be as simple as a few thoughts, a recollection of a cherished experience, or an expression of how you feel about her in your own voice and everyday language. Find some unique cards or use personalized stationery. You can even use that plain, lined notebook paper.

Take the time to write down how you feel and then share those personal words. Make that critical deposit into her emotional bank account. How could you make her day by committing your thoughts about her in a simple, personal note?

## CHRIS'S TAKE

Taking the time to handwrite a note or letter to your spouse is the foundation of friendship. Sharing your inner world with your spouse for the sake of deepening your connection is known as *love mapping*. All of us have a vast cognitive space, full of thoughts, hopes, dreams, and desires. The unfortunate part about that space is most of it is never spoken or relayed to our spouse. Through time this creates emotional disengagement and can even be the cause of divorce. Couples divorce over conversations they never had but should have had. Letter writing is a great way to update your spouse on where you are as well as increase their knowledge of your inner world.

All couples experience various life and marital stressors. In relationships where there are detailed love maps, each person has a pretty thorough sense of the other's inner life. When this is the case, the couple has a greater chance of weathering the storms that will undoubtedly try to hinder the couple's progress.

A psychologist by the name of Arthur Aron wanted to find out if he could make people fall in love.[4] A couple would ask each other questions for ninety minutes and then stare into one another's eyes for four minutes. Amazingly, it worked, and that is because each person asked the right questions and listened to each other's answers. These couples were essentially creating love maps, which provided those invaluable guides to each of their inner worlds.

All of us have hopes, dreams, desires, anxieties, and more. Go ahead and share those with your spouse, and watch the magic happen.

# 3: SHOW A LITTLE RESPECT!

I WAS RAISED by Emily Post's sister—the mistress of American manners! Okay, there's no blood relation between my mom and Emily Post, but if you knew my mom, you would think they were identical twins. My mother was painfully aware of the social graces, and she wanted to make sure that I too was aware of the finer points of etiquette and able to deftly demonstrate them in my everyday living. Do you know how to properly eat a bowl of soup? Which way to draw the spoon and how not to slurp? I do. I was the cute little boy who opened doors for old ladies, who learned how to be aware of the needs of others and to politely defer to my elders in most social situations.

While I rolled my eyes and fought against the constant reminders to do what was right and respectful, I am eternally grateful to my mom for instilling these critical values and skills in me. It is so much more than protocol. It is, quite simply, grace and respect.

We may be lulled into a sense of complacency when it comes to showing respect to someone we know and love intimately. It is easy to take them for granted and instead show more respect for the strangers and other distant people in our lives. Action springs from thought, and if we are constantly looking for opportunities to show those we love and care for that we are looking out for them, it can only deepen the bonds of trust and respect we share with each other. With regard to my wife, I do not do these things because she is a woman. It's not that I think she is incapable or inferior in any way. I do this because I want her to know how much I love and respect her, and I want everyone we are with to know that I respect her and that I'm aware of her needs.

In Robert De Niro's directorial debut, *The Bronx Tale*, there is a classic scene that speaks of respect and consideration. A young man is going on a first date, and he has been told by his mentor that he should absolutely open the car door for his date. He goes on to say that if she is worth a second date, she will lean across and unlock the door for him before he walks around to get in. He opens the door, then begins to walk around, hoping she will reach across, and . . . success!

One of the small things I have always done for my wife, or any woman I am with, is to respectfully stand up any time they leave the table or return. It is a fine point of recognition. It says "I see you, and you are deserving of respectful attention." There has not been a time I have done this that someone has not commented on the attention—looked sideways at their own spouse, questioning why they don't do it for them, or blushed and humbly said it was not necessary to do that for them.

Whether it's holding the door for your spouse or rising in respect for her when she arrives or leaves the table, taking the opportunity to express respect and subtle awareness and deference is being willing to take yourself out of the spotlight and focus on her. Are you looking for those easy opportunities to place yourself second and make your partner in life feel valued and recognized?

## CHRIS'S TAKE

It's through the small things—opening a door or standing up when our spouse arrives—that we create mutual trust. Perhaps more importantly, these small gestures can function as *rituals of connection.* When we do them on a consistent basis, we *create shared meaning.* You might ask yourself why that's important, and we have an answer: rituals bind you to someone or something. All faiths have rituals, and they help followers connect more deeply to their faith. It's the same for couples.

Creating shared meaning ensures a couple views the relationship through a shared lens. It creates walls that surround the couple and protect them from the world's interference. It also opens a shared window through which the couple can view and interpret the world. It creates an anchor for couples, a safe harbor.

In the process of increasing the basis of mutual trust and shared meaning, we are also dissolving issues that feed conflict. The more we trust and the more we are anchored into our marriage, the less we look for the negative, which, in turn, dissipates the opportunity for conflict.

Here are a few simple ways you can create rituals: have dinner with your spouse every night, grocery shop together, pick a special restaurant where you go each year for significant occasions, pray together in the morning or evening, and mutually design ways to celebrate holidays, birthdays, vacations, and anniversaries. While each of these is simple, they are profound in the sense that they add strength to the shared meaning system of your relationship.

# 4: A ROLL IN THE ROSES

ROMANTIC CANDLELIT DINNERS, sensuous scenes of a beautiful couple hand-feeding each other the most delectable bites of food, or that alcohol- and drug-fueled gangster scene where some crime lord uses a gorgeous model as a sushi platter: all way out there and none-too-real scenes that never occur in our own experiences.

My wife and I were recently married and had already tried the romantic whipped-cream-and-chocolate-sauce-by-candlelight scene in the tub—a cold, sticky, slippery mess. We both were laughing so hard at this failed attempt at sweet indulgence that we realized it was not going to be a repeated event!

Like most men, I don't take defeat easily. I was searching for something I could do to break up the monotony and add a little romance to our time together. I read in a magazine article about the soft sensuousness of rose petals and how easy it was to get a few bags from your local florist. Game on! Our first anniversary was coming up, and we would be celebrating with that frozen top layer of wedding cake that you're supposed to have a year later at a nice weekend away together. I wanted something else special. I tracked down a bottle of my wife's favorite champagne and a gallon bag of fresh rose petals. I covered our bed with the rose petals, lowered the lights, and put on some nice music. The scene was set!

Rose petals are some of the softest, sweetest-smelling things you could have next to your skin. They made for an enjoyable, slow, pleasurable time together—one that was tender, sensual, and intimate.

We were challenged to enjoy a roll in the roses. A little forethought and some planning, and we both enjoyed lowering our inhibitions, focusing on each other, and creating some terrific memories.

If the idea of rose petals doesn't work for you, how about some intimate time in front of a fire? It can even be as simple as candlelight in your bedroom (or any other room in the house!) and some soft, easy music. It doesn't have to match the final date scene from *The Bachelor*; just try a little tenderness! Don't worry, it always looks better in the movies.

When was the last time you changed up the routine and created a few sparks?

## CHRIS'S TAKE

Sexuality is certainly a strong driver for men. It's a way, perhaps the predominant way, they express love and feel connected to their spouse. However, there is so much more to sexuality than the physical act. How many of us can say we actually know our spouse's likes, dislikes, fantasies, and desires? How many of us can honestly say we talk with our spouse about sex? When we say "talk about sex," we mean beyond "Do you want to have sex tonight?" These questions are important, and you should be able to answer them in the affirmative. Most couples don't talk about sex. That leaves a vast cognitive space that is never expressed. If we think in terms of *love mapping* and *creating shared meaning*, plus two other key relationship habits—*sharing fondness and admiration* and *making life dreams come true*—all of them apply to sexuality.

Men actually release an attachment chemical called vasopressin during sex. We are literally attaching to our spouses. It's also interesting to note that the frontal lobes in a man switch off during intercourse, while in women the frontal lobes are very active, meaning the female maintains the ability to interpret the interaction through a clear lens, not just one of eroticism.

Sexuality is perhaps the highest form of attachment and connection, and it should be entered into with a vast understanding of your partner and their inner world.

# 5: HER FAVORITE MEAL

I AM A firm believer that sharing a meal is some of the best time you can spend with someone. When you take the mundane necessity of eating and turn it into a pleasurable, enjoyable experience, you are giving a great gift. A smell, a taste can immediately remind us of home, of comfort, or just inspire sheer delight.

When I was growing up, whenever my mom wanted to provide a sense of comfort and satisfaction, she would make a roast chicken dinner. The whole house had that delicious smell that greeted you the second you walked in. It was quite simple, actually—just fresh rosemary and kosher salt on the chicken, roasted until the skin was crispy and golden-brown, served with simple white rice and a steamed fresh vegetable—usually broccoli. Salty, savory, and satisfying. Every time she made this meal, I had a complete sense of being loved and cared for.

We each have that special something that reminds us of comfort, satisfaction, or even sheer indulgence. Taking the time and making the effort to not only figure out what your significant other's favorite meal is but also learn to make it is a real act of love.

One of my wife's favorite meals is steak Diane. I am a cook, and not only do I love to cook food, I love to eat it too! This was a dish I made early on in my restaurant career. It was on the menu at a restaurant where I did one of my first internships, so making this dish for my wife was also a trip down memory lane for me. I pulled out that recipe from the archive, bought all the ingredients, and planned a special evening at home complete with candles, music, and the fancy china. I think Kim liked the recipe I made, but, more importantly, she appreciated the fact that I took the time to do something for her that she loved.

Interest, dedication, and willingness all coming together in one small act of love—now that's a sweet dish! How can you pick up on one of your spouse's favorites and bring it to life?

## CHRIS'S TAKE

Matthew's simple act of cooking Kim's favorite meal covered many of the essential elements of a strong and lasting relationship. First, he knew Kim's favorite dish, which tells us his *love mapping* was up to par. Second, making the meal was an act of *turning toward*, and that builds mutual trust. Third, it created an opportunity for more love mapping to transpire while the two of them relaxed over a nice meal. Fourth, it opened the door to potentially create a *ritual of connection*. Finally, it afforded an opportunity for Matthew to *share fondness and admiration* for his wife.

There is a multitude of ways we can turn toward our spouse thoughtfully and treat them to something nice. Consider taking the time to learn one of the ways she would enjoy being spoiled, and you can surprise your wife with a special effort on your part.

If we take a deeper look into Matthew's story, we see his limbic system at work as he remembers and describes the sights, smells, and tastes of the meal his mother would cook. The limbic system is an area of the brain where all long-term memory is stored, yet it has no sense of time. In other words, we can be in similar yet different circumstances, and the brain will experience the current situation in the same manner as the long-ago one. This is essential to know, particularly if your spouse has suffered trauma.

If your spouse has a history of trauma, it is crucial for you to do your best to be fully aware of its impact on your relationship. In doing so, you will be laying the groundwork for safety for your spouse. If you discover a history of trauma, consider reading *The Body Keeps the Score* by Bessel Van Der Kolk. It's always wise to get professional help to fully work through the impact of trauma.

# 6: TAKE THE INITIATIVE

A RELATIONSHIP IS a partnership, and both partners desire validation that they are contributing in a meaningful way. Being in tune with your partner and willing to occasionally relieve some of her burden is a direct initiative that shows your awareness and appreciation of her contributions to your relationship.

We each tend to have our own formal or informal areas of responsibility. Sometimes we have agreed upon how we'll divide meeting each other's and the family's needs. Even if we have agreed to be responsible for certain duties, it can get tiresome and stale to have to do the same things week in and week out—especially when some of the tasks seem invisible and go without the expression of gratitude.

Men are often accused of missing the finer points and more subtle cues in a relationship. It takes a little more awareness to look for opportunities to be helpful, to pick up the slack and do things for your family or for your spouse that they might normally do. It can be as simple as emptying the dishwasher, putting away laundry, or filling their car with gas and having it washed. Removing a burden or simply doing something that adds ease or surprise can provide a breath of fresh air at just the right time.

It can be difficult to look beyond our own immediate wants or needs. A nap, watching a favorite show, catching up on e-mail, or aimlessly surfing the web all seem worthwhile and like great escapes. We enjoy these things and feel more than justified in doing them for ourselves. It requires discipline, practice, and conscious effort to take the initiative to prioritize your spouse. If you are keeping score and waiting for the other person to do something for you first, you're already missing the point!

It may not be your priority, your hot button, but if it eases their experience in any way, however slight, you are making a deposit in their emotional bank account and taking steps to actively strengthen the relationship. This is not about endlessly taking on more and more of their workload. It is not so much about the magnitude of what is done but the symbol of the conscious effort and dedicated thought that represents your feelings and your commitment to your partner in a fresh and selfless way.

What can you do today to ease your spouse's burdens and show through your actions that you are all-in in recognizing and relieving some of their load?

## CHRIS'S TAKE

Taking the initiative is important in all aspects of life. When it comes to marriage, it's the equivalent of oxygen.

What we see in this chapter is Matthew being conscious and aware of his partner's world as well as the universe of the marriage. By being *mindful*, we are aware of our spouse's needs—of things we can do to help out, things that make our spouse's life easier and send the message "I'm here for you, I'm aware of us and I'll come through." These small acts enhance *trustworthiness*, which is nothing short of the glue that holds a relationship together.

Mindfulness also helps to enhance the *friendship system* in the marriage. Strong friendships help mitigate conflict and manage perpetual issues that might otherwise be harmful.

A simple way to cover the bases on taking the initiative is to sit with your spouse and write a list of all errands, chores, and responsibilities in the home. It should encompass daily, weekly, and monthly tasks. When you agree to take on your fair share based on your mutual understanding of each other's individual and collective work responsibilities, you will be amazed how she responds.

# 7: WRITE HER POETRY

WRITING POETRY IS not only for guys like William Shakespeare. A poem can be a mere collection of thoughts, ideas, feelings, or emotions that you have about the cherished woman in your life. The importance is not in how good a writer you are, but in your ability to communicate your love and adoration for her using simple verse—or your willingness to try.

When you sit down to write a poem for someone, you are truly reaching into yourself and pulling out the truth of how that person affects your life. It is a selfless activity that requires you to focus on the goodness in another person. Writing prose for someone near to you also forces you to spend some time outside of yourself—and today, that is a place where we all need to be a lot more of the time.

I wrote my first poem for my wife when she was my fiancée. Kim was still living in Key Largo, Florida, and I was living in Tampa, about a five-and-a-half-hour drive away. It would still be a month before Kim was to move to Tampa in preparation for our wedding. I had decided to write and send her a poem to let her know how I truly felt about her and the impact she was having on my life. I titled my work "Of Love and Adoration." With it, I enclosed a simple single strand of pearls strung from a necklace that had belonged to my mother.

I mailed the gift and prose to one of her close friends and had her present the gift to Kim the night of her bachelorette party. I waited on pins and needles till the next day to find out how the evening went and to hear what she thought of my dedicated prose. When the time came, she thanked me for the necklace and commented on how nice the poem was. "Nice." "Nice" is to "the earth didn't shake" as "cute" is to "one step above homely."

We didn't talk about it for a while, until one day my wife commented on how meaningful it was to her that one of her friends had written a poem about their close friendship. The subject of "Of Love and Adoration" came up, and I learned that she thought I had copied the poem from some other source. She didn't know I had written it myself. Redemption! My poem now rests in a keepsake box with family photos and other important memorabilia chronicling our time together.

And soon it will be time to revisit that place where I cherish all the wonderful things about the only woman in my life, pull those feelings out, and place them on paper.

Your wife can never experience in too many ways or moments the feeling of truly knowing that you love her. Why not give it a try? If the idea of writing poetry seems daunting, there are many online resources that can help you write your first work. Pick a style of poetry that makes sense to you.

Can you take a step out of your comfort zone and communicate your love in prose?

## CHRIS'S TAKE

Writing poetry is certainly a way to *share fondness and admiration* and to engage in love mapping. It's also a great example of *turning toward*. We have already discussed turning toward, and you will see it as a recurring theme throughout the book. These small acts, consistently repeated over time, create increased levels of trust in the relationship.

Matthew's writing the poem in the first place was certainly an act of turning toward. But there's more to it than that. Turning away came into play too, in a way that could have sunk the relationship if the couple hadn't handled it skillfully. Matthew could've interpreted Kim's response as a turning away, which could have eroded the basis of trustworthiness in the relationship. Matthew's story is a classic example of how each spouse has their own *subjective reality*—their own view of what happened in the exchange. Matthew's subjective reality was "Man, I put a lot of effort into this, and that's all she has to say? I learned how to write poetry, took the time to pour out my soul, and all I received was a casual thank-you?" Kim's subjective reality was "That was sweet. He took the time to find a poem and share it with me."

While this story may seem small, and it had a happy ending, it could have been problematic for both Matthew and Kim. They each could have had unmet expectations that, if not addressed, could have encouraged a turning away and resulted in resentment toward one another.

Finally, we've talked about how couples divorce over conversations they should have had but never had. Thank goodness the conversation took place and a healing occurred in the relationship. This allowed them to move past the time when their realities had not been in sync.

The best way to bridge your subjective realities and turn toward each other again is to utilize a straightforward exercise. It goes like this:

When you _____, I think _____.
When this happens, I think _____.

Both you and your spouse take turns. Simple as it is, this exercise will open up a world you never knew existed and give you an opportunity to adjust your course.

# 8: ADOPT HER PARENTS AS YOUR OWN

MY BROTHER-IN-LAW AFFECTIONATELY calls his new extended family through marriage "the Outlaws." Spouses' parents have traditionally garnered fear and scorn, inspiring an overwhelming sense of dread when one's spouse announces "My parents are coming for a visit!" Our view of this age-old family reality is tainted by a societal expectation of doom and gloom. But not all new parental relationships through marriage are bound to be cursed with pain and misery.

When I got married, I knew I had an active choice to make. The reality of the relationship between me and my newly acquired mother- and father-in-law would be determined not only by my approach and expectation but by my underlying commitment to my wife and our marriage. I was in a bit of a unique position because my mother had passed on right after my wife and I had our first date. Kim met my mother only one time. My father remarried and ultimately adopted two more children, so the family dynamics on my side were a little different than the typical setup.

It was important for me to demonstrate my love for my wife by showing her that I knew she was loyal to her parents and that I wanted to honor her by being loyal and loving to them too. I noticed my wife's father calling his parents, who were still living, Mom and Pop. I adopted these same traditional names for my parents-in-law instead of calling them by their first names. I decided I was going to view and treat them as if they were my own parents.

Deference and mutual consideration became the norms in our relationship. They quickly learned that I not only loved their daughter but also had a deep and abiding love and respect for them. Kim and I opened up our house to them whenever we could, shared vacations and cultural experiences with them, and were always looking for ways we could make their lives a little bit easier and more enjoyable. Even though the expectation wasn't there, I always tried to grab the check when we were out to eat, and I challenged myself to think of new ways we could treat them to fun experiences. I cherish them and treat them as if they are my parents too. Together, Kim and I love showing them how much we appreciate all they have sacrificed for her and their other children throughout the years.

You never realize how much parents love and do for their children until you have your own and understand the commitment and dedication parenting takes. We now had the opportunity to put them in the "honor seat" and ensure that they felt cherished, respected, and loved. I not only gained the woman of my dreams for a wife; I gained two loving parents who recognized and loved me as a cherished son.

How are you demonstrating your love for your spouse by adopting your in-laws and honoring them for their dedicated love for your spouse and your family?

## CHRIS'S TAKE

Our relationship with in-laws can certainly be difficult to navigate, but in Matthew's story, we see something different: a recognition that Kim's parents were meaningful to her and an important part of her life. Matthew didn't just *turn toward* Kim; he turned toward her parents as well. Remember, turning toward is where we build the basis of *trustworthiness*.

While turning toward is a good step, it wouldn't have been complete without *love mapping* and *sharing fondness and admiration*. Matthew chose to engage both Kim and her parents in these ways, and the payoffs were universal.

Matthew had made it a point to make Kim's parents his own, and in doing that, he had to get to know them. He had to begin to understand their story as a couple, as parents, and as individuals. That process opened the door for sharing fondness and admiration. Hearing someone's hopes, dreams, desires, goals, and history naturally brings about a sense of gratitude for their experiences as well as your relationship with them. Let's not forget that love maps were created for everyone in that process as well.

Our *friendship system* consists of love mapping, sharing fondness and admiration, and turning toward. In this story, all three domains are covered for Matthew, Kim, and her parents.

Take the time to sit with your in-laws. (You can do this with your spouse's friends as well.) Ask them their story and the story of the relationship they have with your spouse. You'll begin creating a friendship with them as well as learning about more intimate details of the woman you adore.

# 9: LEARN HER LANGUAGE

I USED TO think I was an expert at picking out gifts my wife would surely love. I would see a piece of jewelry or an outfit I thought would look great on her, and I would buy it thinking I would be exalted for my consideration and my loving act of gift giving. My wife did appreciate me thinking of her, but my thinking gifts were a way to her heart was a big mistake.

Much has been written about the differences between men and women in their style of communication, and in what they rank as most important to them in a relationship. I was introduced to Gary Chapman's book *The Five Love Languages* years ago, and I have used it and gone back to it numerous times to better understand the people I care about and my relationship with them. The premise of the book is that there are five basic ways we all can be loved: through words of affirmation, quality time, acts of service, gifts, and physical touch.[5] We all have varying degrees of desire to receive (and give) each of these types of love.

My wife and I both read the book and took the short quiz (it's available online if you and your spouse are interested in taking it too!) to determine our love languages and shared the results with each other. I had been assuming my wife's love language was gifts, when in fact this was her lowest-ranked way of being loved. Her highest-ranked ways were quality time, physical touch, and words of affirmation.

We now know the most important ways in which we both like to be loved, so we can be more intentional with our affection for each other. From time to time I ask my wife to rate on a scale of 1 to 10 how well I am speaking her love language. If it's not a 10 (and it hasn't been yet!) I ask what I should stop or start doing and how she would most like me to express my love to her. It often also starts a healthy conversation about how well she is filling *my* love tank. As our children got older, we also had them take the test, so we could better understand their preferences.

Taking the time to truly understand someone's love language gives you a little more insight into their psyche and deepens your commitment to your relationship with them. Ask your wife to fill in the blank of this question and see how she responds:

I feel most loved by you when you _____.

Becoming a student of how to better love those you care for is a sure sign of maturity and selfless service.

What active steps can you take to deepen your commitment to and expression of love to the woman you hold most dear?

## CHRIS'S TAKE

There is no question everyone has their own picture of love. The ability to articulate what that picture is presents challenges for couples and can lead to unmet needs. However, when we understand our spouse's picture of what love is, it becomes much easier to connect.

In this story, we see Matthew making the effort to learn more about his wife. We call this *love mapping*. It was also an act of turning toward. Together, these are two essential components of the *friendship system*.

*Men Are from Mars, Women Are from Venus* was a bestseller, and many subscribed to the theory.[6] Research today shows us that men and women are from the same planet, and that planet is friendship.[7] It is the single most important aspect to everyone when it comes to a romantic relationship. This is the magic of Matthew's story. The ultimate outcome was a strengthening of the friendship system.

The fastest and most efficient way to begin working on your friendship system is this:

» Begin to ask open-ended questions in an effort to learn everything you can about your spouse. (That's love mapping.)

» Scan for all the good in your spouse, as well as the relationship, and speak it. (That's sharing fondness and admiration.)

» Turn toward, even in the very small things in life. If you are engaged in an activity and your wife speaks to you, stop what you are doing, look into her eyes, and fully engage with her.

All of these are ways you can learn your spouse's love language: acts of service, physical touch, words of affirmation, and so on. By taking the time to learn more about how she likes to receive love, you can bond with your wife in a more intimate and meaningful way.

# 10: BE HER PRINCE

DOES IT SEEM to you that grand, public statements of love happen only in movies and gushing romance novels? I am living proof that any average, typical, motivated male (or female!) can join the ranks of the hopeless romantics and create an opportunity to publicly declare your love for the one you treasure. It requires a little planning and dedicated thought, but it is well worth it.

After finishing college and graduate school, I was trying to figure out how I was going to apply all the grand knowledge I had accumulated in my studies to business and the beginning of my career. I had met the woman of my dreams, and we had been dating for four or five months. We were really enjoying each other's company and had begun asking more detailed questions about each other's personal backgrounds and our hopes and dreams. Answers to questions like "Is she The One?" and "Have I found my soul mate?" all came back to me as resounding yesses every time. I knew we had strong feelings for one another, and we were being exclusive in our dating. Because of my distracted, slow start in our relationship, I wanted to make my intentions known so she'd have no doubt where I was hoping we were headed in our relationship.

At the time, I was playing polo—yes, the kind on horseback. My team was playing in the finals of a well-known tournament on the east coast of Florida. My bride-to-be (she didn't know it at the time but was about to be left with no choice) was coming to watch the game with her younger sister. We were playing our match on a Sunday, on the main field with the large grandstands. The stage was set.

After warming up and before the match started, I gathered a bouquet of long-stem roses, mounted my steed, and rode out onto the middle of the field and motioned to the woman of my dreams to come out on the field. I dismounted, presented her with the roses, laid a big kiss on her, and told her I loved her. I got back on my horse and rode to the infield to start the game. She was shocked. Everyone applauded.

Later I learned the following story, which I have made my wife repeat, with great delight, again and again when people ask about our relationship. She returned to the stands blushing and smiling, holding her roses, and sat down next to her younger sister. Her sister leaned in and boldly said "If you don't marry him, I will!" Boom, I was on my way to a great courtship that would lead to a unique proposal and a blessed married life at twenty-six years and counting.

How can you unequivocally and publicly declare your love and commitment to the one who makes your heart sing? If you're not comfortable with a grand public gesture, what could you do to show her how you feel? Perhaps it's notes placed all over her home, car, and place of work that make your love visible everywhere she looks. Maybe it's telling her on the hour for twenty-four hours. Maybe it's serenading her at night outside her window. Whatever you are capable of doing, get off your backside today. Plan it and do it!

## CHRIS'S TAKE

In this story, we see Matthew working to learn Kim's *life dreams* and make them come true. When we work to discover our spouse's life dreams, we are deepening our understanding of their internal world. Matthew's gesture is also a significant gesture of *turning toward*, and it served to *create shared meaning*. All of these things are part of what the masters of relationship strive to accomplish.

If we know our spouse's life dreams, it means we have spent sufficient time *love mapping*. It takes time for all of us to be vulnerable and express things dear to us, so when we see life dreams coming true, we can be sure the couple has spent a lot of time cultivating their *friendship system*.

In Matthew's story, we see a classic example of building shared meaning. When we speak of creating shared meaning, we're referring to establishing things such as legacy, values, and rituals of connection.

When you begin to create more intentional, special moments with your spouse, it will have a profound, lasting effect. Each effort, no matter how small, will pay dividends and create conversations for a lifetime.

# 11: LOVE IN ACTION AND TRUTH

ONE OF MY favorite movies is *The Count of Monte Cristo*, based on the 1844 novel by Alexandre Dumas. It is a tale of friendship, love, deception, revenge, and cunning—quite the swashbuckling adventure. It represents so many stereotypical qualities that most men would love to possess and master. In one scene toward the beginning of the film, the protagonist boasts to his best friend at the time, "King's to me, I'm the king of the moment," and the king chess piece is transferred from one friend to another in celebration of their success.

I had always thought it would be great for my wife and me to have a token between us that symbolized the goodness we see in each other and the love we feel for each other. In searching for something, I found the Celtic love knot. This symbol, with its inter-laced knots that seem to have no beginning or end, dates back to 2500 BCE and stands for the love between two people. I was able to find a small, handmade ceramic tile beautifully displaying the knot.

I decided that when I found myself grateful for something my wife had done or proud of her for some achievement, I would dis-play the tile somewhere in her personal space with a short note recognizing her for what she had done and reiterating my love for her. It also became an opportunity for me to just display the symbol for her—anytime and anywhere—to let her know I was thinking of her and show my true love for her.

It's always a good time to celebrate success with your closest friend and create another great opportunity to express gratitude in your relationship. By itself, the act of displaying the piece is a symbol, but it's the words and the fact that we recognize and magnify the good that carries the true import.

How can you recognize your partner in life and communicate your joy as you put them in the limelight and celebrate their success?

## CHRIS'S TAKE

Matthew's story beautifully depicts the concept of *creating shared meaning*. Shared meaning for couples comes in many forms. It can be rituals for going to bed or waking up. It can be part of breakfast, lunch, or dinner; entering or leaving one another's presence; vacations; anniversaries; or, yes, a Celtic love knot.

The importance of creating shared meaning cannot be overstated. These are the things that bind a couple together. These bonds are exceptionally important when the trials of life blow against the marriage. The newly created and then repeated shared-meaning occurrences are the glue that holds the couple together. Rituals keep our primary love and trust relationship, the one with our spouse, intact.

# 12: BEAUTY IN BLOOM

THERE IS A well-known and often cited quote by Anne Herbert: "Practice random kindness and senseless acts of beauty." Buying a woman flowers is one of the oldest, best-known acts a man can do to share some natural beauty and express his love to the woman of his dreams. Doubters may wonder "What has he done that he's apologizing for?" But to many women, flowers are meaningful and have a message that's nothing but positive.

I have come to know that flowers are scientifically proven to brighten moods, boost your woman's happiness, and encourage intimate connections.[8] Wouldn't it be like winning the trifecta if you got all of these results from buying the right bunch of flowers for your lady? If you do it for no apparent reason, then it is actually more enjoyable for her and shows you to be a little unpredictable romantically. By adding this to your repertoire a few times a year, you will be able to stop time for her and invite her to reflect on why she loves you. And, after all, doesn't she just plain deserve flowers every once in a while?

You don't have to always go the full monty with a big bunch of flowers. I found a bud vase with a suction cup that that sticks to a mirror or window. Periodically I will grab a small flower in bloom in our yard or a single-stem rose and place it in the vase with a note on her mirror in the bathroom or by her dressing table. It wasn't anything fancy or expensive, just an honest recognition and communication of the inherent loving thoughts I have for her.

Even the smallest acts of giving and attention can make any woman melt. How can you use some of nature's beauty to reinforce and magnify what you feel for her right now? What are you waiting for?

## CHRIS'S TAKE

There is a saying in the field of marriage and family therapy: "Small things often." Great relationships are not made from seventy-yard touchdown passes. They are made by gaining two and a half yards a play.

In this story, we see how Matthew takes the opportunity to engage in small things often. These are acts of *turning toward* that strengthen *trustworthiness*.

We also see the concept of *sharing fondness and admiration*, which is part of the *friendship system* in a relationship. There are myriad ways a man can express and share his fondness and admiration for his spouse. Matthew giving his wife flowers is a great example. Developing that full and frequently used toolkit is essential.

# 13: MICROWAVE RESULTS

ONE OF THE biggest opportunities I have is to work on my patience: patience with myself, my wife, my children, and all the people who enter my sphere of experience. I often give in to the temptation, in my own mind, to try and cut to the chase and reach the final conclusion. It's an effort to solve a perceived problem or quickly get through a conversation. I want to return to where I was, what I was doing—to my own agenda.

We live in a Crock-pot world, but we all want microwave results. We are bombarded with hacks, shortcuts, and quick solutions in the name of expediency and efficiency. I am all for being effective and not wasting time. However, when it comes to relationships, especially with the number-one on your list, pausing, slowing down, and listening empathically and effectively do more to nourish that relationship than you can imagine. Postponing your own gratification in an effort to invest in your spouse will always pay dividends. This is a theme you will see interwoven into many chapters in this book.

Just a few days ago, I was speaking in passing with my wife. She wanted to get caught up with me on a short list of items so we were on the same page. Some of her list we had previously spoken about, and as she began to speak, I began to process how I could make this quick! After the second thing on her list, I let her know how one issue had been resolved. She lovingly put her hand on my shoulder and looked at me, saying "Would you please just let me speak instead of cutting me off as if you know what I'm going to say?" Like a deer in the headlights, I closed my mouth, focused my attention, and said "Sure. I'm sorry, please continue."

It may sound subtle and insignificant, but learning how to pay attention, listen empathetically, and value what your spouse has to say is not just good communication, it is absolutely essential to a trusting and valued relationship.

How can you increase the quality of your communication with your spouse by dismissing your agenda and letting go of the need to personally solve what she most likely would like to just talk about? Ask her to rate how well she feels you listen to her, and then take personal responsibility to make quality communication a valued, well-worn, and frequently used tool in your relationship.

## CHRIS'S TAKE

Two very important things are happening in Matthew's story. The first is *turning toward*, and the second is *accepting influence*. Here's why they are important.

When we stop and listen to our spouse, we are engaging in the act of turning toward. Remember, turning toward is the fundamental ingredient of *trustworthiness*. Trustworthiness is a heartfelt sense of knowing your spouse is and will always be there. Matthew's act of slowing down and listening to his wife showed her he was there, and that is what great relationships are made of.

To accept influence is to elevate our spouse's opinions and thoughts to the same level of importance as our own. This doesn't mean that we always choose their approach over our own. It simply means we gave it a real look; we didn't dismiss it out of hand. In doing this, you will be mitigating conflict in your relationship.

Here are a few things you can do to accomplish both. When it comes to turning toward, all you have to do is engage your spouse when they speak to you. You can also strike up a conversation with them. The simple act of interacting with your spouse, whether it's responding to them or initiating, shows your spouse they matter.

With respect to accepting influence, when your spouse offers their opinion, stop and listen to it. Reciprocating by taking their idea seriously shows that you understand them and that you're not passing judgement or trying to solve their issue. You don't have to do it all the time. It's the act of really giving it a serious look rather than dismissing it that will register them with and truly have an impact.

# 14: BUCKET LIST

MANY PEOPLE TALK about a bucket list as that elusive collection of things they wish they could do but never seem to get around to . . . sort of like the things they mean to do in that mystical time, "when I retire." In *The Four Hour Workweek*, Tim Ferriss talks about creating a world where we begin living the life we want and desire now, as opposed to signing on to a life of drudgery without joy or bliss.[9]

I have heard my wife say on several occasions that certain experiences would definitely be on her bucket list. After hearing the third or fourth item that would most certainly be on the list, I thought, "Why don't we start doing some of these things now?" My very next thought was how fun it would be to plan to do one of the things on her bucket list and totally surprise her with it.

Let me be bold and up-front when I say it is not about spending crazy amounts of money on grandiose and extravagant things. It is about listening to the person you love and figuring out a way to do something for them that they would love to do. Experiences make memories that will last a lifetime, memories that will be around long after the luster has worn off some purchased gift.

One of the first concerts I remember being dragged to was Celine Dion. At the time, I did not really have an understanding of or appreciation for her as an artist, but she was one of my wife's favorites, so I went. I have to admit I was blown away by her talent, passion, and genuine love for and mastery of her craft. I was dancing and singing and having a pretty good time with my bride. So, fast-forward a few years, and she mentions that it is on her bucket list to see Celine Dion perform in Vegas before she stops doing her show. I know I have to figure out a way to make it happen.

I began to plan, using every trick in the book to pull this together without breaking the bank. I used frequent-flyer points for the hotel stay at the Bellagio and a companion airfare "buy one get one" option through my credit card company. I had to just eat the full ticket price on the Celine tickets, since I couldn't find any discounts there.

The most beautiful part of the trip was that it was a total surprise to Kim. I arranged childcare for our kids while we were gone, cleared her calendar of any obligations, and made it so she could be away without any concerns or responsibilities. You have to understand that my wife is a planner and that she is not accustomed to shooting from the hip or doing anything on the spur of the moment. So, the evening before, when I announced what we were doing the next day, she was in shock. After lots of questions and what-ifs, shock blossomed into excitement, and she began to pack for what turned out to be an incredible long weekend together. Great memories, loads of fun, and, most importantly, an opportunity to fill her love tank and cross one of those things off her bucket list.

What can you do today to plan and execute something that is on your partner's bucket list? Take those first steps with a little abandon and make it happen.

## CHRIS'S TAKE

In Matthew's story, we see a lot relating to the infrastructure of a solid relationship. The most important things are *making life dreams come true* and *turning toward.*

Making life dreams come true is part of the *shared meaning system* in a relationship. Shared meaning is the mutual lens through which a couple views their relationship as well as the world. Simply put, it provides a joint purpose to life. This buffers couples from the inevitable ups and downs and helps stabilize them in rocky times. By planning an expedition to help your wife achieve or do something that is important and relevant to her hopes and dreams, you are actively choosing to demonstrate your understanding of and commitment to her inner world.

Turning toward is the very basis of *trustworthiness*; without it a relationship is doomed. Turning toward doesn't have to mean getting tickets to a Celine Dion concert. It can be as simple as looking up from your phone, fully engaging, and speaking to your spouse when they speak to you.

# 15: APPRECIATED BY FRIENDS

WE MAY NOT all admit it, but everyone loves to hear the good in themselves recognized and articulated by those who they hold in high regard.

My wife and I have birthdays just three days apart. She is only three days older than me, yet it is an ongoing joke between the two of us and all our acquaintances that I married an older woman, that my wife is a cougar, that she robbed the cradle. I'm sure you get the picture.

Cooking is one of my hobbies, so we agreed that for our fiftieth birthdays, we would invite a group of friends over for a dinner party. These friends are dear people with whom we have been taking annual four- or five-day trips for the last twelve years. We may not see much of each other during the year unless we're planning the next trip or celebrating the good times from the last one, but when we're together, our time is full of laughter, joking, and easy conversations. Everyone is willing to pitch in and park their egos at the door.

A week before our birthday dinner, I asked each of the five women from the couples we travel with to think of a favorite quality they see in Kim and a favorite time they have experienced with her, and to put it together in a toast for our evening together. They each did a beautiful job of recounting time spent, gathering pictures, sharing fun mementos, and bringing out those qualities of Kim's they cherished most in their friendship. Some of their toasts brought tears to my wife's eyes, and she told me later that she didn't want the night to end because she was having so much fun.

What did it cost? Nothing. Just a little bit of time, forethought, and focusing on what would help illuminate some of the qualities that my wife most beautifully expresses. And the toasts were best received because they didn't have to come from me!

Who are the people most important to your spouse, and how can you creatively invite them to share that appreciation?

## CHRIS'S TAKE

We all have the need for comfort, attention, appreciation, acceptance, security, and support. These are basic human needs, and all needs must be met. We are biologically wired to get them met. When needs are met in a relationship, it thrives, and when they are not, the couple moves into a state of pain. Pain always pursues pleasure, simply searching for relief of the pain.

While this might seem straightforward and easy to pull off, we cannot overstate the importance of acknowledging and meeting these basic needs. You see, if we remain in a state of pain long enough, we will attach to *something*. It could be drugs, it could be alcohol, it could be endlessly checking your phone, but you will attach to something, and that something will become your primary love and trust relationship.

In Matthew's story, we see him meeting his wife's need for appreciation, and appreciation is a close cousin to acceptance—something we all long for. While Matthew was not the one to directly meet his wife's need for appreciation and acceptance, the fact that he orchestrated it was an act of turning toward. You have heard us mention turning toward throughout the book, and it's important to understand that it builds *trustworthiness*. What exactly does trustworthiness mean? It means "I've got you no matter what. I'm always here for you"—something every spouse wants to know and feel resoundingly.

# 16: PRAY FOR HER

GROWING UP, MY mother often told me that the most loving thing you could do for someone was pray for them. It took me a while to understand why this is true and how to do it.

One of my habits is to start my day off in prayer and meditation. I always pray for my wife, my entire family, and anyone else who comes to my consciousness. I pray for their protection, guidance, and inspiration throughout their day, and I think about which qualities of theirs I am most grateful for or appreciate most. This practice helps reset my own thinking about those who matter to me, and it helps me increase the amount of love I have toward them in my heart.

Regardless of your own faith tradition, you can pray for someone simply by choosing to see them with God's eyes. To me, that means I am getting rid of any personal misperceptions about who they are, how they look, or what their intentions may or may not be. Instead, I know that if they were created like me in the image and likeness of God, then they must be inherently good and able to express some of the varied qualities of our heavenly Father!

It is so much more beneficial to focus on and magnify the good in someone instead of what seems to be wrong. Focusing on the negative is a temptation, a bad habit we all must fight if we are going to choose to build up and support the woman who matters most to us.

Our world is full of plenty of heartache and strife. By changing our own thoughts about someone and holding them in higher regard, we can find unity with them, support their healing, and express gratitude for the goodness they embody and represent. How can this not positively affect your relationship with them?

Rather than casually saying "I'm praying for you" or "I'm lifting you up," challenge yourself to be serious about changing your thoughts so you're thinking about them in the most loving and supportive way. Isn't this another deep expression of love and concern? How can you lift up your best friend and life partner in prayer today, right now, and truly see them with God's eyes?

## CHRIS'S TAKE

In this story, we see Matthew practicing *fondness and admiration*. What we mean by that is simple: we look for the good in our spouse and in our relationship, and we magnify and share it.

Here's why that matters. When we are not looking for good, we will scan for the negative. That produces contempt, and when contempt is verbalized, it produces untold negative effects on our spouse. According to research by John Gottman, couples who are contemptuous of each other are more likely to suffer from infectious illness (colds, the flu, and so on) than couples who are not contemptuous. Contempt is the most poisonous of all relationship killers. We cannot emphasize that enough. Contempt destroys psychological, emotional, and physical health.[10]

There are many other adverse consequences of contempt, including anger, depression, and anxiety, to name a few. The major point being, contempt is the "stage-four malignancy" of a relationship and the number-one predictor of divorce. It is something we want to consciously steer clear of.

This should be a wake-up call to all of us. While we might not be happy with our spouse on some specific issue, it is hard to believe we would want them to suffer because of our way of relating to them. The Scriptures tell us we will reap what we sow. In this story, we see goodness and a win for the relationship.

Take the time to write down a list of any and all ways you feel you might have exhibited contempt in your relationship. Then write down the antidotes to each, and begin the process of intentionally acting in these positive, life-giving ways. For instance, if you once told your spouse her outfit didn't look good on her, you could compliment her the next time she wears something you like. This ongoing process will help to eradicate contempt and at the same time set you up for a lifetime of sharing fondness and admiration.

# 17: SELF-CARE

IN ORDER FOR us to bring our best self to what should be our most committed relationship here on earth, we have to continue to grow, stretch, and work on improving and strengthening our own game.

While working in the senior-living business, I became aware of how couples transition through different stages in their lives. I began to see a pattern where one spouse ends up, out of necessity, becoming the primary caregiver for an ill or incapacitated partner. This is a beautiful and expected process, and is often referred to in marriage vows: "to have and to hold, in sickness and health, till death do us part."

While noble, practical, and forseeable, this situation often ends up demoralizing or ruining the partner who has become the caregiver. Being the best, most attentive and loving partner does not mean you signed up to sacrifice your life and identity, figuratively or literally, for the sake of your partner. To be that loving, devoted, and effective husband, you must establish the practices that strengthen your own constitution—the habits that will prepare you mentally, physically, and spiritually to be there in all ways for your wife.

Let me share a few practices that I engage in daily to help me be at the top of my game so I can be the effective and loving husband my wife needs, wants, and cherishes. This is not an exhaustive list of my daily practices but a few key activities that make a big difference for me.

## GRATITUDE JOURNAL

For two to three minutes in the morning and two to three minutes in the evening, I write in a *Five-Minute Journal*. It is a preformatted book that includes a daily quote at the top and then asks the following questions:

> I am grateful for . . .
> What would make today great?
> A daily affirmation: I am _____.

Then, at the end of the day:

> Three amazing things that happened today:
> How could today have been better?

I have been doing this pretty actively for almost three years now, and it has really helped change my focus to what I am grateful for and what is right in my world. (My wife is often the subject of my gratitude and what went right in my day.)

## MEDITATION

I never truly understood what meditation was or how to do it, until a friend recommended I try a ten-day trial on a daily guided fifteen-minute meditation program. I did, and it is now a twenty-minute part of my morning when I focus on calming my thoughts, controlling my breathing, and narrowing my focus to intentional thought.

In my meditation, I recognize that one of the major reasons I am engaged in the practice is to take care of myself and to be more effective and at ease in my number-one relationship. It has helped me quiet the incessant noise and clamor of the outside world and focus on myself and that one person in my most intimate relationship.

## PRAYER AND STUDY

Every week I read and study a different bible lesson with selections from the bible and a companion book, *Science and Health with Key to the Scriptures* by Mary Baker Eddy. These bible lessons act as the impetus for my spiritual growth and often give me a focus for my quiet prayer time. Not only am I working on strengthening my own spiritual/prayer muscle, I am obtaining inspiration to use in supporting my wife in her daily activities and responsibilities, loving her, and cheering her on in her spiritual walk.

What daily habits can you add (or delete) to strengthen your own character and constitution and make you more successful in loving that woman you have chosen to walk with?

## CHRIS'S TAKE

What we see in Matthew's story are *rituals* plus a form of *turning toward*. While Matthew might not be directly engaging with his wife on these rituals, she is the ultimate beneficiary, which translates into turning toward.

Here's why these are vitally important to any relationship: Rituals bind us to things. In this case, Matthew's rituals help bind him to his wife. Couples with a secure bond weather the storms of life much better than couples who do not have a strong attachment. They know they have one another's back.

When we work on rituals, it's also an indication the *friendship system* is working, which produces a *positive perspective* within the relationship. A positive perspective means we see the relationship in a positive light. It's the thermometer of the friendship system. Turning toward, as we have previously discussed, builds *trustworthiness*, and that is the glue that holds everything together.

# 18: BE ACCOUNTABLE

IT IS EASY to dream, set lofty goals, and think about that ideal future state where you are living your best life in the eternal sunshine of infinite possibilities. Then, the reality of never-ending hard work, difficulty, and eventual failure on some level comes creeping back in and tries to monopolize your time. Having some form of accountability and support outside of yourself and your immediate family is an important element to anyone's success.

Over eight years ago, a small band of brothers and I started our own accountability group and named it *Kaizen*, after the Japanese word for "continuous improvement." We meet once a month for half a day, usually at one of the members' home or business. We open our session in prayer (we represent four different faith backgrounds), share a personal victory from the last month, and then take turns reporting on both our personal progress and our business progress over the last thirty days. If anyone has a major issue, they usually brief the group in advance, and we reserve time to talk about it and help the member work through it.

There is a deep level of trust, respect, and "care-frontation" that allows us to genuinely support one another. This helps us each of us maintain accountability to the goals and objectives we develop, review, and assess on an annual basis.

We all have varying religious and business backgrounds and represent some different life stages, but we have in common a deep, abiding love and concern for one another and maintain an objective view of each member's unique personal situation. There is no doubt in my mind that I am a better husband, friend, father, son, and businessman because of the feedback and support of this unique, intimate group. I could call on any of them at any time for help, and I know that they would all take the call!

By opening up yourself to other viewpoints, impressions, and ideas, you can test your own assumptions and be stretched to step outside your comfort zone. We grow most ourselves when we strive to fill others up first.

Break the inertia and start to form those bonds that will ultimately strengthen your own being. What individual or small group can hold you accountable to becoming the best version of yourself that you can be?

## CHRIS'S TAKE

In this story, we see Matthew trying to be the best version of himself not only for selfish reasons but for his wife and family. This is an act of love that resonates with each member of his family, particularly his wife. When we engage in activities like those discussed in Matthew's story, we are letting our spouse and family know they matter, and that is an act of *turning toward*, which enhances *trustworthiness*.

Here's why it matters: Trustworthiness shows an active engagement with our spouse. We could be typing on our computer and our spouse says something to us. Instead of continually typing, we stop and engage in the conversation. That simple act is turning toward, and over a long period of consistent, dedicated effort, the result is trustworthiness.

Every time we think, say, or do something that involves turning away from our spouse, we take a small step of disengagement from them. It may not initially rise to the level of infidelity, but if it's repeated over time, we could unwittingly end up in a downward spiral that ends in disaster. When trust is broken through any form of infidelity, *all* levels of trust are eradicated and the relationship is burnt to the ground. It is possible to rebuild trust and recover the relationship in the wake of infidelity, but it requires deep commitment by both partners and a complete understanding of the trauma that was created.

Sometimes we are blind to our own shortcomings. We can get so involved in the rightness of our own actions, so caught up in self-justifying, that we fail to see our own fading away from what we hold inviolate. Surrounding yourself with wise and valuable counsel—that is, having others who know you and whom you trust to keep you accountable to your highest self—is an indirect but very important form of turning toward.

By continually finding more ways of turning toward, we are actively working on part of our friendship system (which in turn is made up of *love mapping* and *sharing fondness and admiration*). Taking active steps to improve our effectiveness in all areas of our own experience can't help but heartily spill over into our most important relationship.

# 19: THE TWELVE DAYS OF CHRISTMAS

I HONESTLY CAN'T remember where I got this idea, so let's just assume imitation is the highest form of flattery and I am imitating someone's grand idea! Technically, the twelve days of Christmas, according to the Christian tradition, are the twelve days starting the first day after Christmas and leading up to Epiphany on January 6. For my grand idea, though, I did the twelve days leading up to Christmas, with the twelfth day landing on December 25, Christmas day.

The basic concept is that, as in the song, you give some sort of special gift that correlates with the number of the day of Christmas that you are celebrating. So, for the first day of Christmas, one gift, the second day, two gifts, the third three gifts, and so on. Got it? This does not have to be an expensive, elaborate plan, as you might think, but it will require some creativity and dedication, since it is a project that runs a full twelve days!

I made a real effort. I found cool pens, sunglasses, fuzzy slippers, books, jewelry, underwear (yup, I saved this one for one of the higher numbers!), journals, and all kinds of other things. I even found some cool Christmas-themed stationery with unique envelopes and presented her with notes that read "On the first day of Christmas, my true love gave to me . . ." and then inserted the name of the gift, which I had wrapped for her. The point was that for twelve days, she got to look forward to a special gift, a note, and a genuine expression of giving between the two of us that led us together beautifully into the Christmas season.

There were extra benefits for our young kids. They especially enjoyed seeing what gifts would be next for their mom. It also gave me a great opportunity to show my children that I cared enough to do something special for my wife and had a great time doing it!

I have actually done this for my wife twice, and I'm sure it will come around again when I am feeling industrious or she is having a tough time and just needs to know how much I love and cherish her.

My wife surprised me this past year with her own twelve days of Christmas. I had a blast being the recipient of her loving attention and truly enjoyed her creative, dedicated thought. Another great example of reaping what you have sown and personally experiencing the joy of being your spouse's concentrated focus.

How could you plan the twelve days of Christmas (or the appropriate number of days for another religious tradition) for your wife and turn it into an opportunity to share the joy and delight they bring to your life?

## CHRIS'S TAKE

In Matthew's story, we see a few vital relationship structures being tended to. First, we see a *turning toward* in the gifts Matthew is giving. Second, we see a *ritual of connection* forming. Third, we see a future generation being taught how to tenderly care for their spouse. Here's why these are important.

We have discussed turning toward many times, but it's worth discussing again. Remember, when we turn toward, we are adding to the basis of *trustworthiness* in our relationship. Without it there is no relationship. If we do not know deep within our hearts that our spouse is there for us in ways big *and* small, then our relationships are empty and void of meaning.

Rituals, as we have discussed, bind us to people and things—in this case our spouse.

Finally, it's not enough to think of our children as our family. We must have a deep recognition that they are the foundation of our society as it progresses. Also, research shows that when children live in homes where there are distressed marriages, stress hormones are released, particularly adrenaline.[11] The adrenaline attacks the attentional system of the brain, and children exhibit symptoms of ADHD. A sound marriage relationship not only benefits the immediate couple; like a pebble dropped in a pond, it sends resounding, strengthening ripples throughout the entire family structure.

# 20: AN INDOOR PICNIC

IT IS EASY to think you have to go somewhere other than your home if you want to relax and enjoy yourselves. But sometimes, just setting the scene and creating a new expectation gives you the opportunity to relax and enjoy some of the good that's already right there.

Creating a special space in your own home is a lot easier than it sounds. Our first home together happened to have a fireplace in the living room. One night I ordered Chinese takeout, built a fire, laid out a blanket on the floor, dimmed the lights, and put on some great smooth jazz that helped set a cool and comfortable vibe. Kim and I sat on the blanket, shared a fun, easy meal together, and were able to relax and focus on each other. No one had to cook or clean up, and there were no distractions.

If you don't have a fireplace, that's okay—just put out a few candles and lower the lights to create a warm and inviting place you can both relax in. Back then, I wouldn't have had to say "Make sure it's technology free!" But today, you have to be sure you have removed all distractions and prevented interruptions that could intrude on your time together. No need to look up a fact to support your discussion, take a selfie to show others just how cool you are, or update your social media. Just focus on the here-and-now. Look into your loved one's eyes and ask some thoughtful questions that do not have yes-or-no answers.

Since you took the time to set the scene and create a special experience together, why not carry the thought all the way through and prepare some questions for your spouse that will help you learn more about her and her inner world? You could even "set the table" by inviting her in advance to a special picnic dinner together, so she knows to reserve the date and time. I am a big believer in creating expectations, blocking out chunks of time, and giving each other something to look forward to.

When will you take the initiative, commit to the planning, and create some new, fun memories right there in your home?

## CHRIS'S TAKE

In this story, Matthew is engaging in what we call *love mapping*. Of course there are many other relationship qualities we can glean from the story, but love mapping wins the day.

Here's why this is important for any healthy relationship: The act of asking our spouse open-ended questions allows us to explore their inner world. It's an exercise in discovery—learning the very things that make our spouse tick, make them sad, make them intrigued, and a hundred other things. It also conveys a deep interest in our spouse's world, which helps to build *trustworthiness*.

Asking questions might seem a simple thing, and functionally it is. However, consistently using the right questions will take you on a journey into the deeper realms of your wife's world. Not only will you learn more about her unique and true identity, you will consistently reinforce to her that you have an unquenchable desire to be her steadfast supporter, her knight. This commitment deepens the trust and intimacy you have, and that solid and robust foundation of trust will help bolster your physical intimacy, too.

# 21: A DAILY ACT OF SERVICE

EACH OF US has something we hate to do, or at least something we would much prefer someone else to just do for us! My wife Kim and I start out every day with our favorite cup of coffee. After years of trial and error, we have found our favorite roaster, we have the right equipment, and I know how to make her coffee just the way she likes it. Kim is quite capable of making her own coffee, but I have chosen to make and bring her first cup of coffee each and every day.

I am an early riser, and I truly enjoy getting up a little bit before everyone else in the house and having my first cup of coffee in my favorite chair while I have my morning prayer, study, and meditation time. I also make Kim's coffee for her and either take it to her once she's up or make sure it's ready for her when she comes down to start her day.

It's something small, but something I can do for her each and every day to show her I am thinking about her and that I want her day to start off with something from me. I have been doing this for at least the last fifteen years, and it is a great daily reminder to me to recognize and cherish the good I have and see in her while I am going through the routine of this small task.

What daily, small, selfless act could you start doing for your spouse that would lovingly demonstrate your focus on and commitment to her?

## CHRIS'S TAKE

In Matthew's story, we see many things, but the most profound is *rituals of connection*. As we've discussed, rituals bind us to each other. They provide the glue that holds it all together. They give meaning to our relationships and are a continual reminder of why we love our spouse. Rituals motivate and move us.

We also see *turning toward* in Matthew's story. As you now know, this concept is important with respect to building *trustworthiness*, which is a vital part of our *friendship system*.

Turning toward can take the form of an act of service. In Matthew's story it was making a cup of coffee, but it can be a variety of things. A friend has filled his wife's car with gas their entire marriage, and that simple act of turning toward has created untold benefits in their marriage. Each time she sees that full tank of gas, she is reminded of her husband's care and his intentional provision for her. The point is to be purposeful. We encourage all men to pick a specific act they can intentionally do each and every day for their spouse.

These acts are certainly nice things to do, but there's more to it than that. You are creating a ritual as well as turning toward. Each of these enhance the friendship you have with one another. The friendship system paves the way for in-depth connection in the relationship. These simple acts of service show your spouse that they are on your mind and that you are willing to continuously invest in them. That is a tremendous way to build a healthy and loving relationship without even speaking a word.

# 22: LOVING TOUCH

THE POWER OF touch is profound. It can give reassurance or comfort, help bring a needed calm, or tell someone without words that they are loved and cared for by somebody.

As I mentioned in chapter 9, "Learn Her Language," Gary Chapman's *The Five Love Languages* is a good introduction to some ideas about how you can learn what someone else's love languages are so you can work to better fill their love tank. Since I learned that touch was one of my wife's top love languages (and mine too!), I've known that she appreciates having her face or arm tickled, her head rubbed, and even a back massage if she is so lucky.

Years ago, early on in our marriage, I found one of those how-to articles in *Men's Health* magazine. It was an illustrated, step-by-step guide on how to give a proper foot massage. It was about ten different steps in total and took about fifteen minutes per foot.

I decided to get all of the needed elements—the soaking tub, the Epsom salts, the special foot lotion, and a copy of the guide—so I could follow along and give Kim her first official foot rub. Needless to say, it went incredibly well, and as I was almost finished with the second foot, the quiet snores began to fill the bedroom! Over the last twenty years, we have traded back and forth in giving each other this same relaxing, selfless gift.

Whether you are feeling low, tired, sore, under the weather, or maybe just a little stressed out, being the recipient of focused, intentional loving touch like one of these foot rubs can bring incredible relaxation and calm. It's important to give it without any expectation of reciprocity, immediate or otherwise. It's also important to give it joyfully and willingly, since all of your feelings and emotions will most definitely be felt by the person receiving your selfless act of service.

When can you schedule that dedicated time and give the gift of your loving touch to the person who matters most to you?

## CHRIS'S TAKE

In Matthew's story, we see *physical touch* as an act of love and selflessness. Physical touch has all kinds of benefits. To begin with, it calms the brain. Jim Coan, Professor of Psychology the University of Virginia Affective Neuroscience Lab, has done extensive research on hand holding. He found it helped those suffering with PTSD open up and share when their spouse held their hand. His research also showed hand holding quieted the brain when research participants were placed in an MRI machine awaiting a shock.[12]

Matthew described how his wife would slip off into a secure sleep while he massaged her feet. Of course it's relaxing, but the effect on the brain speaks volumes. There are numerous other health benefits to physical touch, which include improved functioning of the immune system and slowing the release of cortisol, a hormone responsible for inflammation, insomnia, and heart disease.[13] Gentle, reassuring physical touch like hand holding can make all the difference in calming a fearful brain or just quietly letting your spouse know "I am here for you." It can be a simple way of creating shared meaning.

By actively caring for his partner and truly looking out for her best interests, Matthew was demonstrating his love and care for Kim. Relationally, we see a turning toward, and that increases our trustworthiness metric. If you're looking to improve your overall relationship with your spouse, physical touch is a great way to go about it.

# 23: THROW A PARTY

WE MAY NOT all like to be surprised, but who doesn't like a good party? Especially one thrown in your honor with all of your favorite people.

About sixteen years ago, my wife and I were working on remodeling a home that would give us the opportunity to graciously host a lot of friends or family on a beautiful piece of property with plenty of room. Kim grew up in the Florida Keys, and some of her closest and dearest childhood friends still live there with their families. One day, Kim said she felt like it had been a while since she had been able to get together with all of her "Keys sisters" and she'd love to plan something fun. I smiled and nodded, knowing I had an open door.

I was able to get six of her closest friends to come up for a surprise long weekend. I planned some fun activities, including special meals in and dinners out, and I made it so none of the women would have to worry about working or doing anything but relax and enjoy each other's company the entire weekend.

I couldn't have done it alone, and couldn't really afford to hire anyone to do it for me. I was able to call my cousin and close friend Blair in for the weekend to help me and be my sous chef for the meals. All of Kim's friends were in a social sorority together, so, to gild the lily, I decided to have the sorority name embroidered on some nice robes so they would all have something to hang out in and to remember the weekend by.

It took some planning, and it was a lot of work, but the sheer joy and excitement that my wife expressed during and after the weekend made it all worthwhile. I also got to know some of her close friends a little bit better and began to understand why they were so special to her.

I was able to pull this off because I had paid attention to details. I honestly listened to what was important to my wife, and I was willing to act on it in a tangible, meaningful way. It doesn't have to be a complex, weekend-long extravaganza to hit home with your bride. It could be getting tickets to one of her favorite music groups and taking care of getting the sitter and having a nice dinner out, or even finding and booking that yoga class she was talking about and doing it with her.

Have you taken the time and made the commitment to become a student of the person you have committed yourself to for the rest of your life? Have you dedicated yourself to giving her that thoughtful experience she told you she was interested in? Start to listen more, smile, and quietly take note of those giving opportunities. You can start building your inventory now.

## CHRIS'S TAKE

Structurally, we see many things happening from a healthy relationship perspective. What stands out most is Matthew's existential quest for understanding of his wife. Matthew discussed how Kim wanted to see her friends and he knew he had an open door. The mention of it is brief, so you might have missed it, but it's crucially important.

Here's why: In order to truly have a healthy relationship with our spouse, we have to understand what's important to them and why. *Love mapping* is certainly a way to achieve this, but so is *intentional listening* for *deep understanding*. Matthew knew how important the Keys were to Kim as well as her friends and family there. Providing a relaxing weekend allowed him to discover why that was so important to his wife, and also to gain a greater understanding of her friends. This not only helped to deepen his understanding of Kim, it relayed to her, "I'm here, I've got you, I know what's important to you." This is a *turning toward* and that adds significantly to the basis of *trustworthiness*.

# 24: WRITE A JOURNAL

THIS IS PROBABLY the longest running and most challenging thing I have taken on in my efforts to become more selfless and aware in my relationship with my wife. It not only produced an amazing deliverable for me to give my wife, but it brought us far closer by requiring me to think about her in an appreciative, supportive way as opposed to a condemning or fault-finding mindset.

One of my closest friends shared a project that he was doing for his wife. He purchased a journal, and for an entire year he strove to write daily in the journal things he appreciated about her that he actually experienced, witnessed, or perceived in their day-to-day interactions. I have heard from countless people that it is good to journal on a daily basis, so I decided to dive in and start a journal like my friend's. I knew if I could follow through, I could personally develop one of the deepest, most meaningful gifts I could ever give my wife.

Kim is a deeply spiritual person and has a strong faith that guides her every decision. She also has a fondness for different styles of crosses and has a few different ones that she enjoys wearing. I was able to find a beautiful, rustic, handmade leather journal with a leather strap that wrapped around it to keep it closed and was anchored shut with a basic, contemporary-style cross. I began by writing the date on one of the journal's small, lined pages. I started each short written piece with a simple title. I usually wrote in the journal in the morning after my prayer, study, and meditation time, when my mind was at peace and focused clearly for the day.

My entries included things Kim said and did for others, for our children, or for me. Sometimes I just noted qualities I saw her express in the normal motions of her day. You would think that after a short while it would become difficult to find praiseworthy things to say about your spouse, but I never ran out of material!

For a little over a year, I wrote almost every day about the goodness in my wife and our relationship. I saw my attitude about her become more loving as I worked to focus on all of the good in her instead of looking for those trivial faults we can so easily get hung up on. I gave my wife her journal on the evening before she was leaving to go see our daughter in college. (It happened to be on our anniversary weekend; that's why it went on for a little more than a year.) She was quite taken aback by my gift and my effort. Her only comment was "That is the nicest thing anyone has ever done for me."

I'm not sure how much of it she's read, since we really haven't spoken a lot about it since. I was tempted to take it personally that I didn't receive gushing thanks or praise, but I remembered that I hadn't undertaken this for myself, but rather out of a selfless desire to do something deep and loving for my spouse.

When can you start writing and reflecting about the goodness you experience in your spouse? Are you ready to create a timeless, personal expression of her goodness that will last a lifetime?

## CHRIS'S TAKE

In Matthew's story, we see *subjective realities* in play. There are always two realities in a relationship, and they are both real. Couples fumble the ball by arguing over these subjective realities. ( "I cleaned the house last Wednesday." "No you didn't. My mom was in town, and she helped me.") In Matthew's story, we see an example of subjective realities with respect to his expectations and Kim's response. Kim's response really could have meant exactly what she said: "This is the nicest thing anyone has ever done for me." However, Matthew's subjective reality was very different. Fortunately, Matthew had given to give, not expecting anything in return.

At the core of this story is Matthew *sharing fondness and admiration* for Kim. This is, perhaps, the saving grace for all relationships. Why? Because fondness and admiration are the cure for contempt. As Matthew continually trains his thoughts toward fondness and admiration rather than contempt, we actually see good health being delivered to his wife.

You might be thinking, "What in the world are you talking about?" Let me explain. Masaru Emoto, a Japanese researcher, found that he could change the crystalline structure in water as it froze simply by taping words to a bottle of water or speaking words to the water.[14] Positive words resulted in beautiful crystal formations, and negative words resulted in sludge-like formations. This is a great example of why we should be looking for the good and speaking it. Remember, our bodies are 60-plus percent water. Given Dr. Emoto's research, imagine the overall health benefits to both Matthew and Kim through this year-long process of thinking and then writing these positive affirmations.

# 25: TIED TOGETHER

WE ALL HAVE symbols in our life that represent both good and bad memories, achievements and failures, happiness and sadness. Whether it's the wedding ring on your finger, a child's favorite stuffed animal, or a worn baby blanket, these special symbols bring out an emotional response that never seems to fade.

One day I was looking on Etsy for a gift for my wife that would provide some deeper meaning and, at the same time, be something we could each have that would link us to each other. I'm sure you've seen those necklaces where a circle or heart is cut in half and each person gets one half of the whole symbol. These are cute (that's one of my least favorite words), but they weren't bowling me over with creativity or significance.

Then I found a husband and wife team of jewelers from Israel who had designed what they called "heart rings." A set of rings had been made so that when the two of them were held up to one another and viewed through the middle, a perfect, complete heart was formed. The rings were made out of ten-karat gold (not too expensive), and the jewelers explained that the woman's ring consisted of the top of the heart, which is more rounded and soft, while the man's ring was the sharper point of the heart, with some harder edges, but together they formed a complete and balanced picture. I was sold.

I ordered the ring set for my wife and me for our anniversary a few years ago. My ring looks a little like a wedding band, and I wear it on my right hand. One look down, and I see my half of the heart. When I travel or am away from my family, I make it a point to wear the ring so I can be reminded of what I have back home and how we are linked together. It's an invitation to form a stronger, more enduring relationship when we're together.

I've even taken pictures of my ring with my phone and sent them to my wife, asking "What's missing?" and then responding right away, "You are!" It sounds a little cheesy, I know, but I love the fact that every time I wear that ring, I am reminded of my wife and our enduring, growing relationship. The rings are really just another symbol that ties us together and makes us think about how the other person complements who we are and makes us more than we are on our own.

It doesn't have to be jewelry or anything expensive. In this book, I've used examples of specific kinds of flowers, songs, pictures, phrases, writing, quotes, and even poems. The more you fill your relationship with meaningful, personal symbols of your emotional ties to one another, the richer, deeper, and stronger your relationship can be.

How can you "tie yourself together" with your significant other and provide both of you with a meaningful symbol of your connection and your appreciation for one another?

## CHRIS'S TAKE

In Matthew's story, we see the two of them *creating shared meaning*. The significance of this cannot be overstated. It's been said that healthy couples create walls and windows that shelter them from the uncertainty of life. They view the world through those shared windows. We can all relate to this. Life certainly has a way of knocking us off our feet, and shared meaning offers a haven of safety and security.

Enhancing the shared meaning system aids in attachment. We all need at least one secure attachment in life, and there is no better place to have that attachment than with your spouse.

There is another powerful relationship concept known as "*US*." It means we make decisions that benefit "US"—the relationship, not just me. When "US" wins, we both win. I can decide to come home at three in the morning, and that might be great for me, but it will be terrible for "US." When we make decisions that benefit "US," it is a turning toward and that enhances trustworthiness in the relationship.

If you feel there is significant conflict in your relationship, a little more clarity might be needed. Consider beginning to write a list, with your spouse, of all decisions that belong to "US"—that is, to the relationship—as well as types of decisions you each feel are your own. The relational clarity this exercise will bring can help to eliminate power struggles and ensure you are both reading from the same playbook on life decisions.

# 26: JUST BECAUSE

THERE SEEM TO be a plethora of occasions throughout our year when we are supposed to celebrate someone for something. A birthday, Mother's and Father's day, Valentine's day, Easter, Christmas, anniversaries, and many others. Don't get me wrong; it's nice to get recognition, praise, and adoration at any time, but it's the best when it's totally unexpected and driven by someone else's motivation to give of themselves to you and not by the date that happens to be on the calendar.

It could come in the form of an act of service, a small gift, a letter, or even a note "just because." What's most important is that someone who cares for you was thinking of you and chose to take a specific action for no other reason than they thought it was something that would be meaningful to you.

It is an amazing place to be when you are the object, the cause and sole reason for someone's loving affection. You feel important, valued, heard, and even validated when someone understands what is important to you and they work selflessly to provide it. Isn't this what is at the center of every strong and valuable relationship?

I have begun to learn that rationality and my own thought of what is important and why does not always translate well into my wife feeling heard, appreciated, and loved. The simple fact of making her priorities mine gives me the opportunity to demonstrate my focus and commitment by listening and responding to what is top of mind for her. I am working consistently to meet all of her needs and act on them, whether they are expressed verbally or unexpressed and merely intuited. When she knows that my motivation for doing something for her is based on my love and commitment for her and not the specific date, she sees my caring for her out of my own desire, not any kind of obligation.

What small, sincere thing could you do today to make that validation, that affirmation, real and tangible for the woman you value above all others?

## CHRIS'S TAKE

In Matthew's story, we see many things, but what stands out most is a *turning toward*. You remember this is the engine for creating *trustworthiness*. Here's why turning toward is so important and how it overlaps many other areas of the relationship.

When we give of ourselves, in ways large or small, it relays the message "You matter to me." Over time and with consistency, the clear understanding of "You're there for me" resonates strongly in the heart and soul of your spouse.

Taking the time to give of ourselves also enhances the friendship system and can reduce conflict in both the "perpetual" and "solvable" realms. *Perpetual problems* could be defined as differences in personalities based on temperaments, backgrounds, and personal experiences. *Solvable problems* are usually about something that is situational; there is not anything deeper involved. We cannot live in gridlock, but we can live in perpetual, healthy conversations that address differences in personal opinion and perception. Learning to lovingly communicate about these issues is the key to a lasting, loving relationship. It can also contribute to *shared meaning* and *rituals of connection.*

No matter how exactly you choose to do it, take the time to consistently turn toward your spouse. The benefits are endless.

# 27: DO IT TOGETHER

IT IS EASY to think of many things you would like to do on your own or with a group of friends. How easy is it for you to imagine a list of fun things you or your spouse like to do that you can plan and enjoy together? I have to be honest and admit there are probably more things in the "activities with the guys" column than things I could do and enjoy exclusively with my wife.

Kim is laser-focused on achievement and accomplishing things for our home and family. Her first choice of an activity together would probably be something that made our home better, more organized, or more presentable to the friends and family we so often host. Only then would she feel good about moving on to something solely classified as fun.

Kim was a litigation paralegal when we met. She is highly organized and calendared, a planner who does not particularly love surprises or shooting from the hip, even on social activities. (Okay, she's very "left brained"!) I have learned what is important to her, so I have learned to compromise and take turns in what we do when.

If it were up to me, we'd be going out on the lake to wakesurf, going for a stand-up paddleboard, shooting sporting clays, or most anything outside and testosterone charged. She is willing to do some of these things with me, and on other occasions, she'll give me hall passes to go on my own or with others who enjoy the same thing. Sometimes, it is the right thing to have an opportunity to do something with the guys—or, for her, with the girls—especially when your significant other has no desire to do the activity that is fun for you.

That said, it's the things we do together that bring us the closest. The walks we take on the trail with the dog, the paddleboard excursions, cleaning out the garage together . . . no matter what the activity is, we always reconnect on what is going on with us and our family.

Remember that courting or dating stage of your relationship? Back then you were most likely much more flexible and willing to be Gumby. If you want to continue to strengthen your relationship, it is imperative that you relearn that skill of asking, listening, and following up. You must be willing to invest time in those things that the most important person in your life values highly.

During your time together, asking thoughtful, open-ended questions will allow you to continue to be a student in learning about your favorite person. The activity is simply the backdrop upon which we have the opportunity to talk, float ideas, and share triumphs and frustrations. Those times of casual sharing and intimacy pave the way to a deeper, more rewarding relationship. It can at first feel like work, but it will quickly turn into creating memories and strengthening the bond that keeps you close.

What activity can you take the initiative to plan together with your spouse that they will enjoy? How can you lay the groundwork for a bonding opportunity?

## CHRIS'S TAKE

In Matthew's story, we see a variety of things happening, but the most important are *love mapping* and *accepting influence*.

Love mapping is a process where we are continually updating ourselves on our spouse's internal world. This goes beyond the simple niceties. Love mapping means probing to learn more about your spouse: their likes, dislikes, concerns, favorite restaurants, hopes and dreams for your children, and sexuality . . . the list goes on.

Love mapping is the foundation of the *friendship system*. It begins the lifelong process of getting to truly know someone—in this case, your spouse. Sometimes we are surprised by what we discover! For example, a client had been sending his wife roses for seventeen years only to find out she loved hydrangeas.

We also see Matthew accepting influence in the sense that he knows what is important to his wife and is willing to sacrifice his own wants for hers. While we traditionally think of accepting influence as giving your partner's *opinions* the same weight and value as your own, Matthew's thoughts and actions exhibit the spirit of accepting influence. Accepting influence is critical to husbands if they want a successful marriage. Here's why: In John Gottman's research, he found that 81 percent of marriages fail when husbands do not accept influence from their wives.[15] A wake-up call for all of us!

In Matthew's story, he discourses with his wife using open-ended questions. That is precisely how we learn about our spouse, and we encourage you to do it. Life is a complex thing, and relationships are part of the complexity, perhaps the most important part. We all experience anxiety at varying levels, in particular when it comes to our relationships. Love mapping, the process of learning more about our spouse through open-ended questions, serves to move us toward secure attachment, and this in turn reduces our anxiety. Research has shown that simply holding your spouse's hand quiets their brain.[16] In other words, hand holding reduces anxiety. A relationship with less anxiety supports both spouses and is an indicator of a stronger, more enduring bond.

# 28:  WHAT MORE CAN I DO?

IT IS EASY to get caught up in the long list of to-dos that often seem to teeter out of control in our daily lives. With the spiraling demands of family, work, home, friends, and even church, it can seem like we must focus only on our own responsibilities if we are ever to accomplish all we have been given (or merely agreed to take on). It can become the norm to shortchange those we are closest to, because they have the best understanding of all we may be trying to achieve, when in fact, those closest to us are the ones who deserve our first focus and our continued commitment to give our very best.

My wife was serving as president of the Parents Club at our pre-K through twelfth grade school. It was a year-long volunteer role that was supposed to be part time, but because of the complexity and magnitude of the responsibility and my wife's overachieving nature in all things she touches, it was a full-time, all-consuming job. With two of our three children still in the home, our household was also never on hold!

My wife was preparing for one of the biggest all-school events and was staying up late at night to get the extra work done as well as rising early to help with the daily demands of family, dogs, home, and our two school-aged boys. She was tired, a bit overwhelmed, and starting to stress out, yet she still felt the obligation to rise early to meet those daily family obligations. One morning, I asked myself, "What more could I do to help relieve some of the pressure on my wife?" I decided to turn her alarm off, let her sleep in, and give her a chance to catch her breath while I handled the morning routine with the dogs, the kids, and the typical start of the school day. A small gesture, but one that came from genuinely asking myself the question.

I received a happy, grateful call later in the morning telling me I had no idea how much she had needed that extra sleep! Now not only did I receive an enthusiastic blessing from my best friend, but I was so grateful to have taken the time to ask myself, "What more can I do?"

Life will continuously throw opportunities our way. Windows of opportunity will open and invite us in. It would be difficult to answer the call on each and every occasion and personally provide everything the person in front of you needed at that moment. You don't have to do it all the time. But what would happen if just once a day, you resolved to step up, to step toward your bride's need in that moment and ask yourself the question, "What more can I do?" You just might end up making her day, relieving some stress or pressure, or simply meeting that unspoken but deep need for support, caring, or affection.

As more of our interactions turn away from self and toward those we cherish, we open up the opportunity to be that blessing for someone else. We become a more active part of a divine economy where we are able to provide another's need while another is able to fulfill ours.

## CHRIS'S TAKE

In this story, we Matthew *turning toward* Kim. We also seem him acknowledge the possibility of *turning away* instead.

As we've discussed, *trustworthiness* is built when we turn toward our spouse in small ways. An example would be to shift your attention from the television to your spouse when your spouse begins to speak to you. When Matthew turned off the alarm so his wife could sleep in, he was turning toward. These might seem like small acts, and in and of themselves they are, but their impact is substantial. From a relationship perspective, they add strength to the foundation of trustworthiness.

In this story, Matthew discusses the idea of getting caught up in our own responsibilities and shrugging off our responsibilities to love and cherish the ones closest to us. If we do this, we are turning away. The result is a decrease in the basis of trustworthiness, and that births betrayal.

When you commit to tuning in to your spouse in the small things of life, you'll quickly see a substantial benefit in the quality of your relationship.

# 29: MAGNIFY THE GOOD

ONE OF THE first management books I remember reading in graduate school was *The One Minute Manager* by Ken Blanchard. This book is a fun, allegorical tale of a young man who wants to learn how to become a great manager. One of the key practices he learns on his journey is a "one-minute praise." Essentially, a one-minute praise consists of recognizing goodness being demonstrated and immediately praising the person engaged in the positive activity in a sincere and specific way. It includes letting the person know how their actions affected you and the company, and that you look forward to more of this exemplary behavior in the future.

This is not just a business skill, but a life skill! Everyone loves to hear what they are doing right. Everyone appreciates knowing that their positive efforts are sincerely appreciated and are having a specific impact.

Blanchard further encourages us to "Catch people doing something right." When it's the person you love most and cherish above all others, shouldn't it be easy to catch them doing something right and magnify their good? Why have we become conditioned to expect the worst in someone instead of their best? Most likely because it is easier to find fault and point out weaknesses than it is to see the inherent goodness, no matter how small, and elevate it to the highest possible level.

Believe me, it is no fun looking over your shoulder, waiting for the next time your spouse is going to zap you for doing something wrong. What if, instead, your spouse was excited to see you each time they saw you coming because of the goodness you magnify in them? This doesn't mean seeing your partner through rose-colored glasses. It's really about being committed to looking for the inherent goodness in them and then magnifying it so it becomes the most important thing between you. We all quickly learn what behavior and actions meet the most positive and upbeat reactions. We also learn how to do repeat performances so the joy and praise keep coming!

In his article "See the Good in Others," Rick Hanson says, "Try to see the good intentions in the people around you. In particular, sense the longing to be happy in the heart of every person."[17] The beauty of this process is that it is totally free. What does it cost? A minute of your time. Like any skill, it must be practiced. When you practice it, you perfect it. Most importantly, it becomes the new norm instead of the dreaded "isolated instance."

Which of your spouse's good qualities will you magnify first? What will you say to her to do this? How can you light up her day with your positive, affirming words?

## CHRIS'S TAKE

In this story, Matthew is tuning in to what is known as *sharing fondness and admiration.* Here's why it's important:

From a practical perspective, who in the world would attach to someone who continually tells them how bad they are or all the things they do wrong? This behavior, scanning for the negative, is the genesis of contempt. It strips the relationship of its vitality. The friendship system is systematically destroyed. There is no *love mapping*, *sharing fondness and admiration* or *turning toward*, which means there is no *positive perspective* relative to the relationship.

However, the opposite is true when we do share fondness and admiration. As in Matthew's story, the intentional act of looking for positive things regarding your spouse is vital oxygen for every successful relationship. It creates a new paradigm of thinking, as well as new neural set points in the brain. There is a saying in the clinical world, "Neurons that fire together wire together." When we are thinking of the positive, that new habit is hardwired in our brain. Neurons are firing together and in turn wiring together, setting the stage for a loving relationship with our spouse.

Perhaps the most crucial element of sharing fondness and admiration is the elimination of contempt. The importance of this cannot be overstated, since contempt is the single greatest predictor of divorce. Look for and think of good, and then speak it. It does far more good when it is spoken.

# : SHARE THE WEALTH

I AM OFTEN reminded that I have only "high-class problems." Usually, it's not that someone tells me this; rather, it's a realization that occurs when I hear myself complaining about how difficult or unfair something is that I am dealing with at the time. It causes me to pause, be quiet, and think, "What am I really lacking in my life?" I have a roof over my head, plenty of food, a beautiful, healthy family, and blessings that are too numerous to count. I am truly blessed.

So how can I spread the wealth further and share just a little bit of my abundance with others in an easy way? I'm sure you've all heard of the encouragement to pay for the person's coffee behind you in Starbucks, and I've done this myself! But, let's face it, most people who regularly shop at Starbucks are not destitute and struggling in their lives.

In our community, there are a good number of less fortunate individuals who are looking for a leg up. Many can often be seen with signs at stoplights, intersections, or on the side of the road. Many of us want to help, but the pernicious thought that goes through our heads when we consider giving them money is "They will probably just use it to buy alcohol or drugs, and I don't want to support that!"

I have a solution! My wife and I heard of a charity that developed hygiene kits they could give away with some essential personal items that might be helpful to someone who was struggling with their sense of home and place in this world.

We decided to do this project together as an opportunity to share some of our blessings in just a small way with those in need. We took our young kids shopping and bought travel-size toiletries, clean socks, and ten-dollar McDonald's gift cards. We packed these items in quart-sized storage bags along with a scriptural quote of love and support. We both carry a small supply of these packs in our cars, and we actively look for opportunities to give them out.

Genuine concern and generosity is always appreciated, and we can even provide a smile and some words of encouragement without any strings attached. Giving out these kits is not intended to solve any great social issue, but it is a positive, loving step in the right direction. It allows us to share from our bounty and help someone else who really needs it.

My family and I support a lot of other causes and people in our community in deeper ways, but we never want to forget the simple, daily acts of civility and kindness that contribute to the happiness of total strangers. It speaks volumes to our three children when they see us roll down the window, hand out a small package, and bless someone who seems to be living such a different life than our own.

Finding an opportunity to give back together helps ground your relationship and focus it on giving to others. There is a great piece of scripture from 1 Corinthians 10:24, Good News Translation: "None of you should be looking out for your own interests, but for the interests of others." Huddle up with your spouse and find a way that together, you can share some of the wealth from your own rich experience to bless someone else. Service above self, done together, can only strengthen the bonds that already tie you two together.

How can you and your partner "put your money where your mouth is" and start to regularly give back just a little of the bounty you possess?

## CHRIS'S TAKE

In this story, Matthew is dialing in on what is known as *creating shared meaning*. The concept encompasses things like creating a legacy, shared values, and *rituals of connection*.

Here's why it's important: As we've discussed, rituals bind people to things. Think of religious rituals and how they help an individual attach to their faith. Within a relationship, rituals bind a couple together. In this story, we see Matthew creating a ritual not only with his wife but with his family as well. It's a practice where they see the world through a common window, which brings shared meaning into their family. This is the type of thing that really holds people together.

As we've discussed, life can be overwhelming at times, and it's in those times that we need someone there for us who has a shared view of the meaning of life. This in and of itself produces an ally, and having an ally in your relationship is more valuable than you know. At the most basic level, having an ally gives us someone to vent with after a hard day. When we feel that our spouse is an ally, we feel confident that we can weather the storms of life. We can guard each other's blind spots. We can stand together on the wall and keep on building what ultimately protects both ourselves and our relationship.

# 31: PAY ATTENTION

WE HAVE ALL heard the adage that we were given two ears and one mouth for a reason: we are supposed to listen twice as much as we talk. We're supposed to make sure our first step is to listen as opposed to trying to be heard. Is this how things go in your relationship? Does your spouse ever say, "If you would just listen to what I am saying!" I know that after twenty-six years of marriage, I still have an opportunity to improve my listening skills in my conversations with my wife.

Is it just as easy as being quiet and letting her talk? That may be a good place to start, but empathic listening involves a bit more than just "not talking." It means listening actively—processing what she is saying, understanding it, and repeating it back to her until you get that smile and the assurance "Yes, that's it exactly!"

Having a genuine sense of curiosity about what your spouse is sharing with you allows you to lean into your conversations and let her know you're fully invested. The payoff also includes increasing the trust level in your relationship, because your wife knows you are committed to paying attention not only to the obvious but also to the more subtle cues in her communication with you. Being on your phone, answering emails, or watching TV while talking don't really count as active listening.

As I began the journey of transitioning into a new career that would allow me to leverage my uniqueness in the service of others, it became apparent that as I was working on publishing this book, I should also begin to develop a podcast. I decided to call this new endeavor *Kickass Couples*, figuring it would bring to life examples of other successful couples, so everyone could understand and learn from their journeys through marriage and couplehood. Since my wife is the star in my journey to becoming a kickass husband (her words, not mine!), I thought she would be the perfect cohost.

When I approached her with the idea of a podcast, she agreed it was a good one—all the way up to the part about her being the cohost. Through further questions, I learned she felt that a costarring role might not be the best fit for her, and that she wanted to understand more about the opportunity before she could comfortably commit to having a leading role. She and I took a two-day immersive class on podcasting so we could approach the opportunity together and see how she could get behind it in a way that allowed her to support me while at the same time honoring her gifts and her unique skill set.

Often, what ends up being most important is the little details that come out in conversation—the things you discover by observing, by just paying attention to what matters to someone else. When you take action to fulfill the needs and desires your spouse has expressed, directly or indirectly, you are showing that you understand.

It's not always about looking for an opportunity to give a gift or do an act of service. It may translate to better understanding how a specific circumstance makes her feel. It may lead you to realize she would appreciate a certain kind of help. It may assure her that you've heard her communicating her frustration with something she is struggling with, and that you're there for her. Effectively acknowledging that you hear, understand, and can respond in a meaningful way to your spouse shows her your willingness to listen and to support her.

When given the opportunity, allow yourself to focus singularly on what she is saying and how she is feeling in that moment relative to what she is communicating. Sometimes, you won't initially get what she is laying out there. Don't be afraid to reflect and ask yourself, "What was she trying to communicate or share with me when she said that?" We all tend to express our fears and concerns in a veiled way, because we are afraid to share our vulnerability and concern.

Are you paying attention to the details, aiming to notice the smallest things, even those she might mention only once? How can you demonstrate just how well you know the person who means the world to you by acting on one thing that is meaningful to them today?

## CHRIS'S TAKE

There are so many good things in Matthew's story pertaining to relationships, but the one that stands out most is the idea of *deep understanding*. Let's see why this is so important.

From a conflict perspective, it doesn't matter who we marry. We are marrying a particular set of problems, and 69 percent of those problems are unsolvable. That's right, 69 percent are unsolvable.[18] The only way we can handle these is through understanding. And by "understanding," I mean a deep, existential quest for meaning and understanding.

Consider the couple who came to my office arguing about a new window they were contemplating putting in their home. At one point, I observed, "It's not about the window," to which the husband replied, "You're damn right it's not about the window. This woman has been trying to control me for forty-five years." I asked him what he wanted, and he said, "I don't want to be taken advantage of." At last, the real conversation began, and the couple was on their way to a deep understanding of what was transpiring.

This is what Matthew means when he discusses understanding. He's not talking about finding the perfect resolution to some particular problem. He's talking about a heartfelt, empathic understanding of your spouse.

Here's a way to come to a deep understanding of your spouse. Write down a series of questions about their life: their hopes, dreams, desires, concerns, anxieties, beliefs, and so on. Once your spouse has answered those, come up with more questions about the answers they have given you, and listen to their responses. Keep going until you feel you understand exactly why those positions, beliefs, fears, and dreams are so important and an integral part of who your spouse is. Paying attention to the little details can lead to that greater understanding and give you clues about what they like and what they need from you on multiple levels.

# 32: TRY A LITTLE ROMANCE

MY WIFE AND I have been married for more than twenty-five wonderful years. Like any relationship (or anything else worthwhile), it takes constant work and dedicated effort.

Whenever we meet someone new and the conversation comes around to "How did the two of you meet?" my wife and I look at each other, and one of us says, "It's your turn to tell the tale!" The story is full of details about how we met. Okay, we were set up by my dad and his wife through their good friends, who happened to be my wife's boss!

It is not an unusual or incredibly fascinating story. It's not one that sounds much different than many other initial meetings that ultimately led to an engagement. What *is* special, however, and what set the tone for my own role in our relationship, was my proposal. Since I come out of the "how we met" story as a late bloomer and something of a slacker who initially dropped the ball, it is important for all to know that I actually finished pretty strong and came through with some good ol' fashioned courtin'! So, here's how I proposed.

My wife and I had been dating for about seven months, and we had talked about marriage, children, careers . . . all the big issues that would have to be worked out if and when we were to decide to approach the idea of getting married. I was scheduled to go down to Kim's hometown, Key Largo, for her tenth high school reunion.

I decided to fly in two days early and surprise Kim in her home with a proposal.

I worked with one of the only florists in her town and ordered about twenty dozen red roses. I had one large hearth-style basket arrangement made and then bought two cases of bud vases so I could literally blanket her home in roses. I completely covered Kim's second-story home (lots of homes are built on pilings in the Keys) with beautiful red roses. I placed the large arrangement on a small table right inside the front door. I even put greenery and baby's breath on each and every step leading up to the front door, so as she came up the stairs she would follow the path of roses. The stage was set.

I heard the crunch of the gravel in the driveway and looked out the window to see my (hopefully) soon-to-be fiancée pulling in! I ran down the hall and hid in her bedroom, holding the ring box in my sweaty, nervous hands. I heard her footsteps pausing on each step, the key in the door, and then the sound of the door slowly swinging open. I heard a gasp of surprise as she took in all of the roses, and then I began that painfully long walk down the hall. I stopped in front of her, kneeled on the folded towel I had put there to save my knee, and asked her to marry me. She grabbed the ring box, began to cry, and gave me a big hug and kiss.

With that proposal, I surely laid the groundwork for what would be a marriage full of romance and surprises—a courtship that I refuse to let die. A proposal is only one of a million different ways you could add a little romance to your marriage. What about considering some of the following?

> » Make a written invitation to your bride for a special dinner date and request that she wear her favorite dress so you can step out together for a night on the town.

» Revel in your relationship in nature. Plan a walk on the beach or through the woods; go for a paddle board, kayak, or boat ride on the water; or hit a local trail, park, or other natural wonder.

» Make a daytime reservation at one of your nicest local hotels and have lunch in the hotel room through room service. What happens for dessert is up to you!

Whatever activity you plan, think back to when you first met and were dating, before you got married. What were the qualities that attracted you to her initially? Organize your thoughts. Be specific and complete, and prepare to tell her how and why you fell in love with her.

How can you sow a little romance into your relationship by doing something unusual or atypical that will create one of those lasting memories for you and your spouse?

## CHRIS'S TAKE

Matthew's story is certainly one that inspires all of us, but what we want you to see is *positive sentiment override*. Here's why it's important.

It's all about a couple's *friendship system*. Remember, the friendship system consists of *love mapping*, *sharing fondness and admiration*, and *turning toward*. When these are part of a relationship, the result is that the couple has a *positive perspective* relative to the relationship itself. Positive sentiment override is created when good memories and feelings crowd out the not-so-good ones. If the friendship system breaks down, couples will find themselves in the *negative perspective*—which, left unattended, will result in *negative sentiment override*.

The idea that Matthew can look back on his wedding proposal with a warm heart and fond memories tells you volumes about the relationship. When a couple comes to me for therapy and tells me a story like this one, I know there is hope for the marriage. Why would that be? The answer is simple. When couples accumulate the negative, they can reach a point where they can't remember any positive. A complete rewriting of history has taken place. Where there was once good, evil is assigned. Their interactions become skewed, and the relationship is doomed. In this story, we see the exact opposite. Matthew has fond memories of that special day, which translates into positive sentiment toward his wife.

The effective way to accomplish all that is discussed in this chapter is to focus on the friendship system. You can do this by practicing love mapping, sharing fondness and admiration, and turning toward. We have shared what each of these looks like in previous chapters, so you should be good to go. If you are still a little uncertain of what these are, you can turn to the glossary for a clear definition of each.

# 33: BE, DO, HAVE

SO MANY PEOPLE get it wrong. Their focus in life is centered around what they want to have. They spend most of their time pursuing things that are temporal, short-term, and ultimately not designed to bring lasting satisfaction and fulfillment. When it comes to the realm of your most important relationship, what do you want to have? If you are focused on having a happy, cheerful, and adoring wife; a white-hot sex life; or various other states of relationship which may seem to be the ideal, you are going about it backward. If you are focused only on your desired end result, then your goals and mission will be defined by what you want and not what is best for your wife and your relationship.

If you want to *be* a better husband, you must *do* the things that will demonstrate a deep, abiding love for and understanding of your spouse, and then you will *have* a relationship filled with more satisfaction, fun, and happiness.

Think about a target with three concentric circles. The smallest, central ring (or the bull's-eye) is the "be" portion of this model. The next ring is the "do," and the exterior ring is the "have." If we are starting at the core of who we are and who we want to be in our relationship, the "be," we are beginning with the end in mind and determining who or what we want to be before we move on to the "do" portion in the next ring. Action proceeds from thought; the "do" follows directly from a clearly stated "be." Once the "be" and "do" are determined, the "have" is merely the result of the successful execution of the first two elements. When we choose to start with the "have," we can't help but be molded by temporary, less meaningful things.

If you want to be a better listener in your relationship, you can commit to empathically listening to your spouse and seeking to understand her needs and concerns *without* trying to offer suggestions or solutions. When you can effectively restate her concerns back to her, you have taken a step to *doing* what you need to do to invest more in her and your relationship. You will then *have* a relationship where your spouse feels listened to and heard, which will increase trust, intimacy, and affection. Aren't those three things you would like to see more of in your relationship?

How can you define a core value that is a critical part of your relationship, and then temper your actions to better demonstrate that value in what you think, say, and do? Go for the bull's-eye and start out with what you want to be. Try it once, and you will see a deeper, more committed, values-consistent you emerge in your relationship. You can continue your growth as someone who will be more balanced and more attractive to the most important person in your life—and to everyone else who comes across your path.

## CHRIS'S TAKE

There is so much we can learn from Matthew's story. Up to this point, we have focused on straightforward things you can do directed right at your spouse—tangible things they can feel. In this story, we see the personal growth element that is less visible but essential for all of us. It is a necessary relationship habit.

Why is this important? Think of a car. The engine is a system, and that system needs proper fuel. If we put water in the gas tank, we'll wreck the engine. The same is true for all human beings. We are a system—a system that has spiritual, physical, and emotional components. The entire system must be tended to if we are going to operate at full capacity. When we think of our relationship, it's important to keep in mind that if our system is not functioning properly, things will get off track. Our engine will be misfiring.

We have been encouraging you to take time to grow the *entire* you. Remember, this is a marathon, not a sprint. You are identifying habits that need to be replaced, altered, or magnified. Be patient with yourself and your spouse. As long as you are steadily adding more tools to your toolbox, you will continue to grow in your expertise and your effectiveness.

THERE IS A terrific old movie called *The Princess Bride* that was quite popular when I was in college back in the eighties. One of the key sayings that came out of the movie was what the farm-boy-turned-swashbuckling-hero would say to his princess every time she asked him to do something: "As you wish." With a smile on his face and genuine love in his heart, he responded to her this way each and every time.

I made the mistake (just one time) of saying "Yes, dear" to my wife when she had asked me to do something for her. She let me know, in no uncertain terms, that her ex-husband used to say that to her and she truly hated the expression. We both had watched *The Princess Bride* many times, so I decided to change my response to "As you wish." I make sure there is genuine respect and love in my thought and voice each and every time I say it, and I only respond to my wife in this manner—everyone else gets "My pleasure!" instead. The first time I responded to one of her requests this way, she lit up and exclaimed, "Ooh, I like that!"

Whether it's by text, e-mail, voicemail, or right in the moment, I choose to find a fun, humorous, but tender response to the typical questions and requests posed to me by my wife. It allows me to have a special moment each and every time I can affirmatively respond to help, support, or merely answer a question.

It is easy to turn the mundane into the sublime when you choose a unique and genuine response to your partner that they will recognize and receive in a positive way. Here are a few examples of how some other men have chosen to lovingly or playfully respond to their wives' questions and requests:

1.  One great husband says "A la orden," Latin-American Spanish for "At your service!" delivered in a sweet, loving way.
2.  Another friend says, "I would love to help you with that. Do you know why?" His wife responds playfully, "Why?" And he replies "Because you are *priceless*!"
3.  One of my friends, who is a pilot, simply responds "Wilco!" which communicates receipt of the request and willingness to comply.

How can you custom-tailor responses that will make your wife feel like she is always tenderly cared for?

## CHRIS'S TAKE

Matthew's story is a classic example of *turning toward*. Certainly there are other things we can glean from the story, but the most important, structurally, is turning toward.

In previous chapters, we have spoken about turning toward as it relates to the growth of *trustworthiness*. Let's look at it from a different angle this time. Think of a time you made a request of your spouse and received a "no" or a response that wasn't relevant to the topic at hand. As a man, you probably translated that as disrespect. Our spouse might do the same. In Matthew's story, we learn that his wife was upset by her ex's habit of saying "Yes, dear." His sardonic tone made her feel *turned against*. Obviously a belligerent response does nothing to enhance the friendship system or accrue trustworthiness.

Relationships are about "small things often," and in this story you see a classic example of something small but profound. Benjamin Franklin once said, "Little strokes fell great oaks." This is one of those finer-point skills that can have a significant impact when added to the rest of your inventory.

# 35: SING TO HER

THIS IS A tradition that started in the most unusual way. I was visiting my then love interest (future wife) in her hometown of Key Largo, Florida, for the first time. She had taken me to one of her favorite local dive seafood restaurants, and we had just sat down to dinner. It was still early, but the karaoke DJ was just beginning to set up for the evening, and the place was pretty empty.

The DJ asked us if we wanted to sing anything. I immediately responded with a "Hell no!" Kim smiled and said "Why not?" I told her the microphone was all hers, but she too declined. The DJ then proceeded to play a favorite song of mine by James Taylor, "Your Smiling Face." Even though I didn't have a mic in my hands, I turned to Kim and belted out the entire song at the top of my lungs. (Good thing the music was nice and loud!) My singing and the meaningful words lit up her face. She truly appreciated my efforts at a modern serenade. The magic really happened the next time I heard the song. I was by myself, so I decided to call her and sing it to her all over again!

It is now a tradition that no matter where I am—in the car, an elevator, an airport, or a store, or jamming out at home—whenever the song comes on, I call her. Even if she doesn't pick up, I leave a singing-serenade voicemail.

Identifying and remembering those moments in time—the places and experiences that bind us together—and then celebrating them with that specific song can remind us of that special moment in time and make it feel like we are in it again right now.

Is there a song that has that special meaning to you or your spouse? If you had a theme song, what would it be? How can you use it to celebrate your relationship?

## CHRIS'S TAKE

Matthew's story is an example of creating *rituals of connection*.

Remember, rituals are things that bind a couple together. They bring meaning to their shared life. They create a framework to operate from and have the potential to bring meaning and purpose into any moment within a relationship.

Matthew's belting out songs—whether in public or on a voicemail—lets his wife know "You're my girl," and that, my friends, sets the stage for a shared window to view the world.

This can also be interpreted as a *turning toward*, which increases the basis of trustworthiness and enhances the attachment between a couple.

# 36: ASK THE RIGHT QUESTIONS

IT'S EASY TO get sidetracked by the daily demands of a family, our job, and maintaining some semblance of order in our household. The questions we ask our spouse may be limited to "need to know" (and "need to survive the day") questions—ones that often fail to open up dialogue about feelings, concerns, wants, and basic desires. I'm talking about mundane exchanges like "What do you want to do for dinner?" or the unimaginative "How was your day?" It's easy to fall into this trap, and it can strain the ties that keep us aligned and happy in our most important relationship.

Asking the right questions is the key to getting out of the "chore zone" and back to being intimate life partners. It's not just a way to gather information that might be useful to you; it is a golden opportunity to let your spouse know you hear her and value her deeply.

Think of a good time to have some quality communication with your wife. Pick a low-stress, relatively relaxed moment. It might be walking the dog, doing the dishes, once the kids are in bed, or first thing in the morning, if you are both up and have some quiet time together. Then ask her some questions that will open up the channels of communication and yield some intimate details about where her head is right now. It will also signal to her that you are interested in how she is feeling about any number of issues.

Your mission is not to swoop in and diagnose or fix her ills. That may be a trail you can pick up later, but first, seek to understand. If you just can't seem to find time during the course of your day, save some good questions and include discussion time in your next date. Good communication can help you feel closer to each other. There's also a chance at improved intimacy!

Consider using some of the following questions, or write a list of your own.

> » What do you think about the amount of time we spend together?
> » Name your least favorite household chore.
> » How well am I filling your love tank?
> » What's one thing I have never done for you that you wish I would?
> » How did we make each other smile this week?
> » Describe your perfect day.
> » What dreams and desires do you have that we have never discussed?

After you talk, take notes to remind yourself of where your partner is at that specific time. If you want to take a deeper dive into the power of questions, I encourage you to read *The Right Questions* by Debbie Ford.[19]

How can you make room in your day to allow quality communication time? How can you use deeper, open-ended, and thoughtful questions that will not only bring you closer to your spouse but allow you to learn more about their intimate hopes and desires?

## CHRIS'S TAKE

Asking the right questions is a great way to engage in *love mapping*. The idea is that we park our own thoughts and go on a journey of updating our hearts and minds on what is happening in our spouse's internal world. This is the basis of the *friendship system.*

Here's why it's important: We often hear that men are from Mars and women are from Venus. As a therapist, I know this is a myth. The research tells us the most important thing to both men and women is a good friendship.[20] They want a good friendship but forget how to create it.

Well, the first step in any relationship is getting to know someone, and we do that through conversation—specifically by asking a lot of questions. When we do that, we are love mapping. We are also turning toward, which builds *trustworthiness.*

I always ask couples to remember the days when they spent countless hours together simply talking, and after they left each other's presence, they jumped on the phone to talk more. They were learning all about each other, and that is love mapping. Chances are they were also sharing *fondness and admiration,* and the mere fact that they were engaging each other in conversation shows a turning toward. These three elements are the foundational components of friendship.

Matthew brings up something else that is important. By parking his own agenda, he shows his willingness to set aside his own self-interest and actually take genuine interest in his spouse.

Here's what you can do to help start or strengthen the process of love mapping. Go to the app store on your phone. Type in "Gottman Institute." You'll see an app called "Card Decks." Download it; it's free. Inside you will find multiple card decks on varying topics with thousands of questions you and your spouse can explore. You'll be surprised by how much you don't know about your spouse, and you'll be working on all aspects of the friendship system.

# 37: ASK HER FRIEND'S COUNSEL

HAS THE THOUGHT ever come to you that it might be time to do something special for your wife? It could be giving a gift, solving a problem, or even taking on one of her responsibilities so she has a break. You could always ask her what she'd like, but sometimes it's nice to be able to just provide the right thing.

So how do we figure out what that perfect thing might be? We can step out of our own need to provide the solution and talk with someone who knows her well and, perhaps, in a different way than you do.

As men, we struggle with the urge to solve every problem and to come up with every solution on our own. The "I can do it myself" complex is not just reserved for young children; it is also worn as a badge by many men. I am certainly in the front of that line! I struggle with seeking wise counsel from others before acting.

I've discovered that one of the most effective ways for me to learn more about my wife's desires or state of mind is to confer with one of her close friends. I'll even check in with my daughter, now that she is in graduate school and on the same page as my wife in many ways. Women just approach issues so differently from men. When I have an idea for my wife, it has been extremely helpful for me to reframe it with the input and feedback of another woman.

I consider myself pretty savvy and aware, but I still seek out the sage, alternative viewpoint of someone else who has built trust and respect with my wife. This also goes a long way to opening lines of communication with people who might then feel freer to give you a heads-up about concerns or observations they have about your wife and her state of mind.

Who can you use as a resource and a sounding board to get some valuable feedback on your one and only? Who can help you refine your ideas about how to show your love and support for your spouse?

## CHRIS'S TAKE

In this story, we see a thinking beyond the self and a spirit of *accepting influence* that can help any area of a relationship. Matthew was willing to look outside of his own thinking and find another authority. There are times when our own personal resources simply fall short and it's beneficial to seek out knowledge that we do not already possess.

Here is why that is important, structurally, for a relationship. Simply put, we can be missing the mark and not understand why. Sometimes we lack the knowledge; other times we are just too close to the trees to see the forest. By asking a close confidant of our spouse what they think, we open a new lens through which we can view our spouse. This helps us know her more deeply.

Remember, we are always on that existential quest for meaning and understanding. Sometimes, this quest will take us outside our relationship to close confidants of our spouse. In Matthew's story, we see him taking this step. Think of all the relationships your spouse has and the volume of information you can take in by reaching out to her family, friends, and children. If we are going to understand our spouse, if we are truly going to gain an accurate view of their internal world, then we need to venture into all aspects of their life.

Here are a few ways you can accomplish this. Start with your spouse. Set aside time to ask probing questions about their hopes, dreams, aspirations, and goals. Then reach out to her family—her mother, father, brothers, and sisters. Then reach out to her friends, coworkers, and mentors. Ask all of them what they know and think of your spouse, what they believe is important to her, what hopes and dreams she might have shared with them. The idea is to gain as much information as you possibly can about who your spouse is.

By doing this, you will go a long way in building friendship, intimacy, and trust. You are lovingly communicating your desire to get to know her in a deeper, more intentional way.

# 38: HOLD THE RIGHT THOUGHT

WHATEVER WE CHERISH in our thoughts and focus on in our efforts becomes who we are. How critical it is, then, to be aware of where we are turning our gaze and to be certain that what we are working toward will fulfill a greater purpose. Above all others, shouldn't your spouse be the focus of positive, loving thoughts?

It is easy to get sidetracked and lured away to meaningless, empty, and even destructive thoughts about the person we consider our best friend and confidant. It requires discipline, focus, and an ever-evolving plan to be intentional with our thoughts about our spouse.

This is something I am working on right now. I had gotten into a bad habit of magnifying the mistakes, the bothersome little things that my wife sometimes did (or the things she did not do that I wished she had). I allowed each one of those "mistakes" to fuel the fire and further affirm an ill-held opinion about who she was to me. Man, what a losing proposition!

Instead of feeding this destructive downward spiral, I decided to turn the habit on its ear. Now I take the opportunity every day to look for, recognize, and magnify my wife's innate goodness in my own thought. I insist on seeing and affirming her goodness to myself. I have reinforced this behavior by adding a new activity to my morning ritual. During my prayer, study, and meditation time, I journal about ten things I am grateful for and three people I wish to send love to in my thought and activity. I make sure my wife is always on my gratitude list as I reflect back and write about my current experience.

I am searching for opportunities to magnify the good, the innate qualities I fell in love with, and to rebuke, forget, and ignore the others that would try to attach themselves to her. This means not bringing her mistakes and missteps to light or reminding myself (or her) of previous failures or shortcomings. What good can possibly be accomplished with that behavior? I am doing this to be crystal-clear and focused in my own thought about what I love about her, so she will tangibly feel my loving thoughts and her love tank will necessarily spill over.

You must become a better guardian of the way you think about your spouse if you want to take your relationship to that next level. Joseph Murphy, an Irish-born New Thought author, says it this way in his book *The Power of Your Subconscious Mind:* "Know that belief is a thought in your mind, and what you think you create."

How do you think she will relate to everyone else when she feels completely, extremely cherished and loved herself? It can't help but overflow onto everyone else around her—friends, family, and everyday acquaintances.

How can you create the best internal dialogue in your own thought, and then show and tell your wife what you love about her? Not once, not once in a while, but as often as anything, even ever so small, comes to your mind.

## CHRIS'S TAKE

In this story, we see the concept of the *positive perspective*. As discussed in previous chapters, cultivating the positive perspective will keep us from slipping into contempt. You already know how vicious contempt is, not only to the relationship but to your spouse's health.

Think of the times when you've nurtured a critical spirit toward your spouse, a scanning for the negative. Remember how that made you feel? Now think about how it must have made your spouse feel.

It is critically important to learn how to focus on the good in your spouse, and in turn to speak it. This will produce untold rewards for you, your spouse, and the relationship. Remember, when you scan for the positive, you are training your brain to make *positive comparisons* as opposed to negative. Positive comparisons simply mean we view our spouse more favorably than an alternative, particularly another woman. Committing to seeing your spouse in a positive light breathes new life into both of you individually and into your relationship.

# 39: WORK ON IT AND IN IT

HAVE YOU EVER thought about how much time you are willing to dedicate to improving or mastering activities that you love or that are good for you? Eating and diets, exercise, playing an instrument, video games, or any other hobby or activity? How about TV? How much time goes into keeping up with your favorite shows? Is it possible that you spend more time on TV than on your number-one relationship?

It's amazing. We put untold effort and countless hours into dating, wooing, courting, and making sure the "special someone" wants to spend the rest of her life with us, and then, once we're married, many of us go on autopilot, and our gaze shifts to other, "more important" things. I admit that in the past, I have been guilty of exactly that behavior. I think we all have. I have fallen into the habit of taking the most important person in my world for granted. I especially forget about the maintenance to keep the wheels on, balanced, and in alignment. Why am I so surprised, then, that when we are on the highway and going fast, and something tough hits us, the wheels fall off?

In any relationship, it's normal for there to be a steady ebb and flow. One partner will seem to take the lead, holding the reins in guiding and leading the relationship, and it is all right to allow yourself to be the recipient of your partner's loving efforts. The problems seem to arise when one partner, and possibly both, takes their hands off the wheel and allows the relationship to go on autopilot.

We were made to be in relationship, and we were built for love. If you are not approaching your relationship as a grand adventure where you get to (not "have to") be in relationship with this most wonderful person and where your number-one job is to be dedicated to the maintenance the relationship needs to keep humming along, then you may just be headed for that cliff.

If you haven't noticed by now that I am a dedicated, lifelong student of my best friend and partner, then you haven't been paying attention! Throughout this book, I have given you ideas and examples of how to build up, invest in, and dedicate yourself to that beautiful woman who also said "I do!" There is no magic number of hours or amount of investment that is exactly right for everyone. That right balance consists of your dedication expressed verbally and, more importantly, demonstrated through what you think, say, and do. If these three are not in accord, your spouse is bound to pick up on that less-than-optimal attitude and approach.

You've got to develop your plan and then work to implement it on a daily basis. Whether we're talking a plant, a garden, a business, or your most important relationship, only consistent and intentional thought leading to regular action demonstrated over time will ensure a healthy, thriving relationship.

Are you flying by the seat of your pants? Are you just throwing stuff at the relationship wall, hoping it will stick? Or have you made an organized, concerted, and dedicated attempt to holistically and consistently love and support that woman who has the ability to leave you speechless with her love, intelligence, and beauty? Consider using our Kickass Quotient assessment (you can find this free, dynamic assessment tool online at matthewphoffman.com) to see how you are doing in the thirteen key areas of your relationship. Then, take the next big step and ask your spouse to evaluate you as well. The conversation that will ensue will help give you a great overview on stellar performances as well as opportunities for growth and development. The humility to ask your partner how you're doing and get scored on your efforts is a great start in understanding how effectively you are loving and supporting her.

It is often said that others can tell what we love most by what we spend most of our time on. How can you let your dedication and commitment to your relationship with your wife be a bright beacon for all to see?

## CHRIS'S TAKE

When Matthew challenges us to think about what we're spending our time on, he's really encouraging us to dedicate ourselves to cultivating the *friendship system.*

We have all experienced times like the ones Matthew describes . . . times when everything else is more important than our relationship. We *turn away* from the most important (human) relationship we have. The result is a decaying friendship system. The *love mapping* ceases, which means we no longer seek to know more about our spouse. The *sharing of fondness and admiration* grinds to a halt, and *turning away* is commonplace. The friendship system has withered away, along with the *positive perspective.* Without friendship, we have nothing. Conflict is everywhere, and *creating shared meaning* isn't even on the radar.

It's essential that we stay focused on strengthening our friendship with our spouse. Don't be afraid to really evaluate your own performance, and invite your wife to do the same. Those face-to-face, loving, honest, no-punches-pulled conversations are critical to the health and well-being of your relationship.

Never give up on being your wife's best friend. She needs one as much as you do. The positive results are as effective as an antibiotic to failing health and as strong as rocket fuel for a vessel breaking free from the earth's atmosphere.

# 40: LET'S TALK ABOUT SEX

WE TALK ABOUT the movies and shows we like. We talk about that last excellent meal in great detail and share the tastes and flavors that sent us into gustatory overload. We might even share an intimate and fondly held memory of what she was wearing when you felt most attracted to her and really turned on by how she was carrying herself. But when was the last time you had a detailed, open, and honest conversation with your wife about your favorite sexual experience together?

It is tough for me to trace back to the roots of why or when we became so afraid to openly and regularly talk about our sexual desires, needs, and preferences. There is plenty of research that shows couples who have open conversations about sexual issues are more satisfied with their relationships.[21]

So, what's the risk? Most people feel very vulnerable talking about their sexual needs and desires. But there's also a risk in *not* talking about it. If we say nothing, gloss over the real issues, and refuse to talk or listen to our partner about what we each need and desire, will anyone's needs be better met? I admit that talking about sex is not something my wife and I used to do on a regular basis. Once we committed to working more intentionally on our relationship and strengthening its core, these conversations became a more frequent and comfortable part of our relationship.

This is not a conversation you want to surprise your spouse with. Asking in advance to talk about it or planning a time gives her, and you, a chance to prepare and think about some of your own concerns. My wife and I had our first such conversation over a glass of wine watching the sunset: relaxed, casual, and stress free. I tried to frame most of my statements using "I" as opposed to "you," in an attempt to make sure it didn't come across as me pointing an accusatory finger. I asked about her needs, preferences, frustrations, and desires.

Wouldn't you like to know what your wife likes best when it comes to sexual relationships? Do you know? Does she know what *your* desires are?

A willingness to be vulnerable and selfless is key. In one of our discussions, I learned from my wife that what was most important to her was how we were relating to and intimate with one another right after making love. This was a time when I felt we were done and I could move on to other things, but she was desirous of being close physically and continuing to talk, share, and appreciate each other through close, loving touch. My sense of our intimacy was expanded by my new understanding of her desires. I also learned that as our friendship outside of the bedroom deepened and became more trustworthy and respectful, our sex life became more passionate and fulfilling.

Many men think that intimacy is defined as sex. Intimacy can certainly be achieved and experienced through sex; however, sex is just one of many ways to be intimate with your partner. Intimacy really means any process that helps you feel truly seen, known, and connected to your partner. It's about deepening your affection for each other. Connecting emotionally with the woman in your life and truly knowing her innermost, closely held feelings will certainly bring you to a new level of intimacy. Having regular conversations about your sexual intimacy will connect you with your partner in a deeper, more meaningful way. To paraphrase the words of Stephen Covey, if you seek first to understand your spouse and their needs, you will then pave the way for your needs and desires to be understood. A win-win, right?

It's time to start turning the tide on what was once thought awkward and unapproachable. When can you plan to have that next, or first, conversation with your most-loved one about her sexual, intimate needs and desires—and yours?

## CHRIS'S TAKE

Sex is certainly a topic that's important to all men and women. In Matthew's story, he speaks to the essential element of discussing sexuality with our spouse: likes, dislikes, desires, fantasies, and more. He also speaks to the broader issue of intimacy, which is at its most profound when it comes to sex. We want to create personal sex, not impersonal.

Here's why this is important. Throughout the centuries, sexuality has come to be known as something bad. We have attached numerous social norms, mores, and taboos that have no basis in God's design for sexuality. Sex is something as wholesome and pure as taking a walk. Nothing deviant about it. Nonetheless, we've been taught it was the original sin. Young girls are told "don't," as opposed to "wait," which attaches a negative and tainted meaning to sex. Not a good match on the wedding night, when the guys are running across the room like Conan the Barbarian!

But I assure you, sex was not meant to be off limits; in fact, both women and men are meant to take pleasure in it. There's a great example of this in the book Song of Solomon. I know, shocker, right? Who would have thought about a detailed description of sex in the Bible? The important thing to know is throughout the book, he builds his bride up. The end result: she bellows, "Make my garden breathe."

The most important point about sexuality is to make it personal. Typically, sex is very impersonal. The husband is getting his needs met while his wife is staring at the ceiling. That is not what sex is about. It's a deeply personal connection. The way to go about creating personal sex is to build all the relationship habits we have been discussing throughout this book. When we think of sexuality, the same principles apply. When you and your spouse are committed to developing a wonderful sense of intimacy through all the ways that are not sexual, your lovemaking can begin to expand in enjoyment and deepen in meaning. This is an effort to create personal sex, eye to eye and soul to soul, as opposed to impersonal. When relationships are strong and couples feel connected, they feel connected in their sex as well.

Make it a point to think of your spouse, not just yourself, when it comes to sex. Meet her needs, not just your own. Most women will complain that their husbands only think about themselves in the bedroom. It's vitally important to be interested in, and selflessly focused on, *her*—not only in the bedroom but in all the elements of her day-to-day life.

Here is a way for you to enhance the sexual love map of your spouse. Write down what you want to know about her sexually: her likes, dislikes, dreams, fantasies, and desires. Find a quiet time and a quiet place, and then begin to ask her the questions, so you can take that deep dive into the inner world of her sexual identity.

# 41: SAY THANK YOU

THANK YOU. GRACIAS. *Arigato. Merci. Grazie. Mahalo. Danke sehr.* It doesn't matter what language you speak; saying "thank you" is critical in your daily recognition and expression of gratitude. When I have the opportunity to speak to groups, I often ask, "Who here feels overappreciated for the work they do?" Usually, no hands go up in response.

Being valued is one of the most important needs of the human psyche. This age-old desire is inherent to our own internal validation of who we are, and it's the reason people often give as to why they stay in a relationship or job, or choose to leave. Receiving validation for the good we do through a simple, genuine "thank you" makes us happier and healthier, too, according to a UC Berkeley study.[22]

The easiest way to adopt a daily habit of expressing gratitude is to look for those opportunities in the moment to recognize your wife for the good she is doing for you, your family, or your community. It could be taking a moment face to face to smile, say "thank you," and relate the specifics of your gratitude. It could be a text, a brief written note left on her dressing table, a Post-it on the steering wheel of her car, or a note written in lipstick on the bathroom mirror. (Make sure you don't use that expensive favorite brand of hers!)

Be mindful that you don't allow your expression of thanks to become the kind of generic "good job" we blindly throw at someone for merely proving that they are breathing. Tell her how she affected you with her efforts and what you specifically appreciate about her undertaking. If you can add a gentle touch, a squeeze, or even a hug, you will be physically reinforcing what you say, and the impact will double.

How can you intentionally verbalize your gratitude for the daily good—big and small—that your wife is bringing to you and your relationship by smiling and uttering those sweet and tender words: "Thank you"?

## CHRIS'S TAKE

In Matthew's story, we see him intentionally expressing gratitude to his wife in order to create a positive habit of mind. Over time, this creates a *positive perspective*. As you've already learned, when *positive sentiments* dominate, the relationship feels good to both members of the couple. Matthew has shown us why this is important and how you can do it too.

All of us enjoy a compliment. It feels good when someone takes notice of us or our actions. Your body actually releases dopamine, and the effects of that are pleasure and satisfaction. In life, we have two positions, a positive habit of mind and a negative habit of mind, and they will generalize into all of our relations. In other words, if we focus on and call out the positive with our spouse, that frame of mind will not only benefit them but will spill over to our children, extended family, coworkers, and friends. The same is true of the negative habit of mind. As human beings, we clearly respond much more favorably to gratitude and thankfulness, as opposed to criticism or doubt. But don't take our word for it; just think about what *you* respond most positively to.

Choosing to live in the positive frame of mind sends a simple but profound message to your spouse: "I see you and your efforts, and I am grateful."

# 42: JUST NIP IT

SINCE THE 1600'S, there has been a gardening practice that has turned into a much-used metaphor: to "nip it in the bud." Growers would frequently "nip," or pinch off, the buds of a plant in order to stop them from developing and to force the plant to put its energies into more productive uses. This practice transferred to the literary term that urges us to squash something before it gets established and "blooms" into a mature state.

In your day-to-day conversations with your spouse, each of you may say things that raise the hairs on the back of the other's neck. We all bristle at things that do not ring true. Nobody likes to be called out on something they have said or done. One of our natural tendencies when we are called out is to retreat and disengage. When we're confronted with what we see as a false notion, we may strike back defensively with our own accusation or condemnation. Sometimes, we simply turn away, swallow the bitter, and say "mea culpa." None of these responses is healthy, and we can't maintain any of them for the long run.

When we find ourselves offended or defensive, it is important for us to first seek to understand what our spouse is saying to us and why. We can then ask what they see as the best outcome to counteract or change what they just described. You can then affirm that you understand how the circumstance or situation truly affects them. It is never easy to be reminded of our own shortcomings and called out on them. If the message is sent with love instead of as a personal attack, we can immediately step toward the situation and respond out of love. If the delivery was not winged with love, you can gently let her know how it was received and see if that was her intention.

On a Saturday morning many moons ago, my wife declared, "There's only four things on my list for you to do today!" I didn't know if I should be glad there were just four or think of what my list was going to include for her! Instead, I paused, calmly thought about what she had just said, and lovingly engaged in continued conversation. I shared with her that I was happy to prioritize some things that were important to her; however, when I was being told what I needed to do instead of asked or lovingly requested, it was difficult for me not to feel put upon and respond negatively. I relayed that if she had lovingly put her hand on my shoulder and said "Sweetheart, there are a few things I would love to get accomplished in and around the house today. Would you mind taking the lead on getting these done?" I would have had a much more positive, calm, and receptive feeling about her and the request.

If you choose to shoot straight—to say it now, to say it with truth, care, and conviction—you can avoid assumptions that lead to misunderstandings. You will prevent the rock pile of accumulated issues from becoming so large and looming that it results in an inevitable avalanche that is certain to overwhelm and destroy.

Do you have the habit of leaning into small, expressed issues and concerns with your partner in an effort to redirect or alleviate them? How can you build the muscle of being an open, honest, and tender communicator with your bride? How can you "nip in the bud" those resentments and miscommunications that try to take root and, if left unchallenged, wreak havoc in your relationship?

## CHRIS'S TAKE

In Matthew's story, we see an episode where he initially took his wife's pronouncement as *criticism*. The natural response is *defensiveness*. Here's why it's important to avoid both of these tendencies.

John Gottman, the world-class relationship researcher, has identified four predictors of divorce: criticism, contempt, defensiveness, and stonewalling. (*Stonewalling* is when we disengage—for instance, we get to a certain point in an argument where we stop speaking, stare out the window, or walk into another room.) Gottman calls these the Four Horsemen of the Apocalypse. When these are present when a couple argues, there is a 94 percent chance the couple will divorce unless they get help.[23]

The good news is, Gottman has also found the cure for each.

> Criticism → Soft Startup
> Contempt → Sharing Fondness and Admiration
> Defensiveness → Accepting Responsibility
> Stonewalling → Practicing Self-Soothing

Here are simple ways to defeat each of the four horsemen. When it comes to criticism, always think of a soft startup. The idea here is to stay away from "you." If you do this, you'll go a long way in eliminating criticism. We see Matthew engaging in a soft startup, which neutralized his own dose of criticism and the defensiveness that could have ensued. The cure for defensiveness is to accept responsibility. In other words, if you didn't take out the trash, don't shoot back with something your spouse didn't do. Simply say, "You're right. Sorry about that."

*Contempt* is the number-one predictor of divorce, so we need to pay close attention to the cure. *Sharing fondness and admiration*, the act of looking for the good in your spouse and your relationship, will eliminate it. Finally, the way to deal with stonewalling is to practice *self-soothing*. You don't have to become an expert in deep-breathing exercises. Just pick up a magazine or a book and read for thirty minutes. That will get your brain working again, and you will be able to return to the situation and engage in rational conversation. Be sure to tell your spouse you're not ignoring her but rather taking a little time to calm down before continuing the conversation.

# 43: THE IMPORTANCE OF "US"

WHEN YOU MARRIED, "me" and "you" became "US." It all started off with a loving, supportive relationship where you focused on and paid attention to each other. Over time, many things—including inattention, neglect, and stressful life events—can take their toll and start to unravel the fabric of your relationship through conflict, unmet expectations, and a breakdown in communication. It really is a slow death that occurs over time, until one or both of you have reached your limit and you ask yourself, "How did we end up here?"

When you started your marriage, you brought all of the good intentions with you, but you did not necessarily have a lot of real-life experience that was going to allow you to keep building, caring for, and renewing that relationship that is supposed to be for life. Deliberately dedicating your time and effort, being present, expressing appreciation, listening, and learning to be a better communicator are all essential to any successful relationship. But being a master of all of these skills and more will not make that relationship bulletproof.

If you want to build your relationship into something that will flourish and stand the test of time, then you've got to have a bilateral commitment to intentionally investing in the success of your union, your "US." Attending weekend marriage seminars, watching a video series, reading books together, and committing to unfiltered, loving, and deep conversations will all help keep your relationship strong and satisfying. The "set it and forget it" approach does not work in your number-one relationship.

My wife and I are investing in our relationship and working together to continually improve it. This sometimes means changing my priorities and being willing to do and try things that are not familiar, or might not otherwise have been my priorities. Working on "US" does not mean abandoning the self and becoming a doormat. It *does* mean making sure that each member of the couple knows the other's needs, wants, and desires and then prioritizes making them happen.

In addition to investing in "US," it is critical that you, as a couple, fully understand and communicate about how your day-to-day decision-making process works relative to "I," "you," or "US." Conflict can easily arise when one partner in the relationship feels discounted by the other because their spouse made a decision on their own that the partner felt belonged to the relationship—to "US." Coming to a clear agreement on how you plan to approach decision making is key. In other chapters, we have discussed the importance of a mutually agreed upon division of domestic duties. Similarly, there should be open discussion and agreement on how you will process individual and collective decisions in your relationship. This includes a shared understanding of which decisions fall into each category!

Like an olive tree, which can produce fruit for over a thousand years if well cared for, your relationship will thrive and bear tremendous fruit if you invest in all of the varied care that's needed to establish strong roots and healthy branches. The number-one question is, are you willing to take yourself out of your first response (that is, do some personal pruning), and instead be willing to become a student, an aficionado of the woman you said "I do" to?

What can you do that will allow both you and your spouse to invest in and strengthen your relationship? How can you initiate discussion to learn how your spouse approached decision making before you were married and how she sees it as you move forward together? Understanding the process she experienced growing up, in her family of origin, and in her life before you will help you navigate this process as you grow together. Your investment will pay big dividends if you continue to pour in more of the same love that helped you start your most meaningful relationship.

## CHRIS'S TAKE

In this story, Matthew introduces us to the concept of "*US*"—the unit that consists of both partners in the relationship working in concert. "US" *is* the relationship. It's not me; it's not my spouse; it's the essence of both of us. Here's why that's important.

In every couple, both partners need to continually be looking for how they can score a victory for the relationship. This may include individual decisions by each partner, but, as Matthew points out, they need to look at activities, decisions, and opportunities that will strengthen that marital bond and equip their relationship to last as long as that well-cared-for olive tree. It's about prioritizing shared experiences that will increase your understanding of each other and the effectiveness and longevity of what you are building together.

Let's look at how the concept of "US" applies to decision making. There are always decisions that belong to you as an individual, ones that belong to your spouse, and ones that belong to the two of you collectively. An example of a decision that belongs to you is what you wear each day. A decision that belongs to your spouse would be what they eat for lunch. A decision that belongs to "US" would be where to go on vacation.

These principles seem pretty basic, but they are violated on a regular basis in relationships. For example, suppose a friend says, "We're having a cookout out Friday night. Why don't you guys come on over?" You respond, innocently, "Sure." This is where the problem begins. What the two of you would do on Friday night was an "US" decision. It involved both of you.

Let's put it into a different scenario. You decide to cut a deal, and then you tell your boss about it. To your surprise, he's not happy. Why not? Because it wasn't your decision to make. You see, power struggles arise when we don't respect where decisions lie. You can commit to the cookout on Friday, and that decision might be good for you, but it might not be good for your spouse, and you won't know unless you ask her. Making the decision without her is not good for "US." When we make decisions together that are good for "US," everyone wins.

Don't make the mistake of overlooking this simple principle. Your commitment to making "US" decisions instead of defaulting to the often-easier "me" decisions will directly strengthen the foundation of trust in your relationship. This practice of "US" decision making, plus your ongoing commitment to investing in your number-one relationship for the long haul, will act as two more strong cords in the unbreakable rope of a relationship that is made to last.

# 44: THE ETERNAL WOO

WEBSTER'S 1828 AMERICAN Dictionary defines "to woo" as "to court solicitously; to invite with importunity." Does this sound like something you are doing on a regular basis with your wife? Okay, most of us most likely employed some of these "wooing" techniques when we were in hot pursuit of our brides. For some reason, men feel that the contest for winning a woman's hand in marriage goes all the way up to the "I do!" Once they've reached that point, many men hit autopilot and seem to move on to focusing importunately on other things in their lives—and that's a problem!

Guys, we're running an ultramarathon here, not a fifty-yard dash. We're going to go through an incredible variety of terrains and conditions, from mountaintop revelations to Death-Valley trials by fire. You get to choose your approach to the race! Are you going to expend all your energy in the first mile, or are you going to commit for the long haul?

A friend of mine told me that while he and his wife were going through their courting process, they agreed they would not proceed with their relationship unless they both committed to an "eternal woo." Neither of them wanted to give up that feeling of being relentlessly pursued and overwhelmingly desired. They both wished to always feel valued and unconditionally wanted by their chosen life partner.

What consistent little things can you do to remind your wife how much you desire her and want to be only with her? This book is full of examples of things you might do to demonstrate your love. Acts of service are nice and certainly appreciated, but it's your mental game, the way you are thinking about your spouse and your relationship, that drives your relentless pursuit of and desire for her. How have you built—and how are you continuing to build—that active, fun pursuit of the woman you picked to be your one and only?

## CHRIS'S TAKE

What we see happening in this story is the constant commitment to strengthening attachment. The mechanism described is a kind of *turning toward*, a concept we have previously discussed. It's important to remember that securely attached couples don't put the brakes on; they continue their loving pursuit of one another. In his opening remarks to his team as the new head of the Green Bay Packers, Vince Lombardi said, "Gentlemen, we are going to relentlessly chase perfection, knowing full well we will not catch it, because nothing is perfect. But we are going to relentlessly chase it, because in the process we will catch excellence. I am not remotely interested in just being good." If we approach our relationship with this frame of mind, we will experience the eternal woo.

Here's why it's important. You remember that turning toward builds *trustworthiness*, and without trustworthiness, relationships die. Trustworthiness is also the crown jewel of a strong *friendship*, and if we want the "eternal woo," we are going to have to build a friendship with our spouse. As you now know, *love mapping*, *sharing fondness and admiration*, and *turning toward* are the three components of friendship. Love mapping is the process of continually expanding our knowledge of our spouse's internal world. We can achieve that through open-ended questions. Sharing fondness and admiration is simply looking for the good in our spouse and speaking it. Turning toward is engaging our spouse in the small moments of life, like putting your phone down when your spouse speaks to you. If the relationship is going to last and the woo is going to be eternal, then you must build an eternal friendship.

# 45: NO WINNERS

I AM AN incredibly competitive person. Whether it's a game of Horse with my son, a weight-loss challenge with my trainer, or my desire to exceed financial goals for my division in the company, I want to do well, finish first if possible, and certainly try to win the prize.

Nonetheless, I know that competiveness is not always the way to go. I learned early on as a father that I did not need to win in competitions with my kids. (I didn't always intentionally lose, either!) I also have repeatedly learned that my wife and I are not competing for who is the better spouse, who makes more money, who contributes most at home, or who is most committed with any of our three children. We are a team. She can count on me to have her back and support her no matter what. I will not betray her trust, deride her in front of anyone, or allow anyone to cast aspersions on her. I am her number-one fan, her biggest cheerleader; I love amplifying her achievements to anyone who will listen.

Let's talk a bit about redefining "winning" at marriage. It is certainly not about how many years you've been together. Some people choose to stay together because it is the easier, more comfortable thing to do. I know couples who are "together but separate." They live together but share so little that they are much more like independent contractors who have an understanding or have reached a good working agreement. You are winning and thriving in your marriage when you are extremely satisfied and your spouse feels the same way. You are both being heard, attended to, pursued, cherished, and elevated to that number-one spot in the life of someone who promised, before God and witnesses, to be with you no matter what. It is really not that difficult when both partners are committed to working on and in their most sacred relationship.

On a recent drive home with my wife, I grabbed her hand and told her I had something to tell her. She said "Uh-oh!" and smiled. I told her not to worry, and then I explained how I have never been happier in our marriage and how much I appreciated all she was doing to make me feel fulfilled and loved. She smiled and said, "It's a two-way street, and it shouldn't be too hard. I feel really happy for all you are to me, too!" (I then proceeded to get a little teary and choked up myself.)

There it is. Two people, equally yoked and committed to one another in their marriage. It doesn't mean there aren't challenges, arguments, and disagreements. We are not perfect people in a perfect relationship. Human perfection sure seems like an oxymoron. We have just chosen to work at all of those things with a foundation of love, respect, understanding, and selflessness. It means being willing not to win for yourself, but instead to win for your marriage and to lean into the relationship, constantly adjusting course, calling audibles, and being willing to set aside strongly held personal beliefs if it will be the best thing to strengthen your relationship.

Are your efforts laser focused on winning for both of you? Are you always looking for wins that you can both put in the right column? How can you articulate a winning vision for your marriage and then align your actions to make your commitment visible each and every day? It's a paradigm shift you have to make. It can start today, and it will undoubtedly have payoffs bigger than you ever imagined.

## CHRIS'S TAKE

In Matthew's story, we see him setting aside personal agendas in favor of developing the strength of the relationship. We see the building of "US."

In an earlier chapter, we discussed "US" as it relates to making decisions that benefit the relationship, not just you. There is another crucial element to "US," and here it is. Relationships can either be "I-you" or "I-it." In I-you relationships, I see you as *a separate person* with your own thoughts, feelings, and emotions. I honor you as a separate person by respecting your thoughts, feelings, and emotions; I do this by realizing the relationship is not just about me. In I-it relationships, I don't see you as a separate person with your own thoughts, feelings, and emotions. I see you as an object or tool to serve my own selfish needs. I don't particularly respect you; it's all about me.

It would seem obvious that no relationship can survive in a lopsided I-it shape. But unfortunately, many relationships consist of one-way streets and dead-ends. If you are going to be effective in building "US" and creating the eternal woo, then you must realize that your spouse is a separate person and who needs to be seen, heard, and acknowledged.

Here's how you can do it. You've already learned one way: Before making a decision, ask yourself whether the decision belongs to you, to your spouse, or to "US." From there, act accordingly. Another way to build "US" is to appreciate your spouse and recognize their contributions. Back off and let her shine as much as *you* want to shine. If you do these simple things, you will be stepping outside yourself and treating your spouse as a separate person with their own thoughts, feelings, and emotions.

# 46: STAND AND DELIVER

*STAND AND DELIVER* is a 1988 American drama based on the true story of a high school math teacher, Jaime Escalante. For his role as Escalante, Edward James Olmos received a nomination for an Academy Award as best actor. Escalante instructs his class using a philosophy of "ganas," a Spanish word from the verb *ganar*, roughly translating to "win, earn, gain, or desire." Would you like to earn a smile and win a little adoration from your wife every time you see her for the first time each day, or after a time of being separated by work, family, church, or other commitments?

It's about genuine recognition. The simple gesture of dropping what you are doing, standing, and moving toward your wife with open arms and initiating a warm embrace coupled with sweet words is a far better greeting than "Hi honey, I'm home" or a simple "Good morning" as you continue to read the paper, watch the news, or fix your gaze on a meaningless electronic device.

Think about this scene instead: I usually rise before my wife and young son in the morning so I can take care of myself with a little bible study, prayer, journaling, and meditation. If I hear my wife is awake and getting dressed, I grab her that first cup of coffee, take it up to her, and greet her with a kiss and a steaming cup of Joe. (You may recognize this ritual from chapter 21, "A Daily Act of Service.") If my wife comes straight downstairs because she knows I will be driving our son to school, I get up out of my chair, walk to her, and engage in what I described above. If she comes home after being out or enters my office to have a conversation, I stand and engage her in the same loving practice.

I am choosing to stand and deliver an active, physical reminder of my love and admiration for her. She knows she is more important than most any activity I might be engaged in and that I am choosing to acknowledge her and affirm her place in my life. This simple ritual anchors our interaction in a physical, meaningful way. It becomes the smooth runway for a more connected conversation and with my spouse.

What loving, meaningful, unique ritual can you establish with your wife that will be a consistent, steady reminder and yet another way for you to express your love, honor her, and focus on her each time you meet?

## CHRIS'S TAKE

In Matthew's story, we see the intentional decision to build a loving ritual for the first time he sees his wife each day or after being apart for a long period. How does the creation of this ritual feed the relationship?

You'll remember that *rituals* are a large part of the *shared meaning* system. When we discuss shared meaning, we are talking about things the couple has created to say "You matter, and I'm showing you." These rituals help shape their mutual view of the world, a shared vocabulary of how to interact. Rituals bind us together. As we've discussed in previous chapters, healthy families have an abundance of rituals of connection.

Think of a way you can develop a practice that contributes to your shared meaning system. It may be something similar to what Matthew did, or it could be something as basic as rising with a big smile and open arms each time you are "reacquainted" with your wife after being apart, and recognizing her with a meaningful term of endearment. Developing more opportunities for shared meaning will bring rich feelings of connection with your spouse.

# 47: TAKE OUT THE TRASH

IF YOU THINK that by titling this chapter "Take Out the Trash" I'm talking about household chores and the best division of domestic duties, you are wrong! The condition of our mental and emotional households have a significant impact on the health, ease, and clarity we have in our number-one relationship. We can get bogged down in the emotional "trash" relating to our marriage or life in general. If our thinking is clouded by anger, resentment, fear, sadness, or self-imposed isolation, we are severely handicapped. Holding on to that emotional baggage will at best slow us down. At worst, it will totally incapacitate us and halt our forward progress, making happiness nothing but a distant dream.

My coauthor on this book, Chris Cambas, recommended that my wife and I work our way through a video series put together by Richard Marks. Dr. Marks is a seasoned licensed counselor, author, and a speaker sought after by social-service, business, military, and faith-based organizations.

My wife and I worked through the *Enriched Christian Marriage Video Series* and found it most helpful, enlightening, and constructive in our efforts to enliven and strengthen our marriage. One of my favorite activities that Dr. Marks leads his participants through is called "Taking Out the Trash." My wife and I did this, and we have continued to do it. This is what it looks like.

Sit down with your partner in a quiet place, facing each other, knee to knee and holding hands. Look each other directly in the eye. Take turns telling one another the following things:

1. Anything you are **mad** about.
2. What are you **sad** about.
3. Anything you are **afraid** of.
4. What you are **glad** about.

If you are the listener, you are to ask only leading questions to encourage your spouse to tell you more about their statements. As the listener, you are not to ask any of your own questions, pass any judgement, or provide any opinions. Just listen, reflect, and acknowledge. Your role is to provide openings for them to fully pour out all they are feeling. As the speaker, you should feel free to share any emotions on any topic so you can shed the burden of carrying them alone. You draw closer to your spouse by trusting them with your current, personally real emotional state.

Michael Beckwith, the founder of Agape International Spiritual Center, once said, "A relationship is a joint participation in the good of life."[24] This practice of taking out the trash is something you can visit periodically. It's a great way to check in with your spouse on where each of you is emotionally at a specific point in time. Remember, mental closeness is a great form of intimacy, and increased intimacy is always a good thing in your relationship.

When can you next call an audible and ask your bride if you can take out the trash?

## CHRIS'S TAKE

It's easy for all of us to get caught up in our day and in our own lives. Great relationships require a continuing exploration of your spouse's reality. Her thoughts, perceptions, likes, dislikes, desires, dreams, struggles, and triumphs continually inform how she perceives the quality of her day-to-day experience. In Matthew's story, we see an existential quest for *deep understanding* of his wife's inner world. Here's why that's important.

There was a Cold War strategist by the name of Anatol Rapoport. He found that the United States and Russia couldn't get to the bargaining table on nuclear weapons until each agreed that two *subjective realities* were in play and each nation could state the other's subjective reality to their satisfaction. Only after this happened could the two nations make headway on protecting the world from nuclear holocaust.

So it is with our spouse. Before we can ever get to the bargaining table of our relationship, we must embark on a deep quest for understanding of our partner's inner world, and we must let her know that we get it. In doing so, even if the two of you disagree, you can build a sense of empathy and in turn a softness around *perpetual problems* or other difficult issues within the relationship. At a fundamental level, we all want to be accepted. It's a basic human need, and we don't feel accepted if we don't feel understood without judgement.

Here's how you can explore your subjective realities. Pick a particular sticky issue in the relationship and ask the following questions.

> » What do you believe about this issue?
> » Is there a story behind this for you?

- » Why is this so important to you?
- » What do you need regarding this issue?
- » Is there a fear or disaster scenario surrounding this issue?
- » Is there a deeper purpose or goal for you regarding this issue?

Remember, you're only going for understanding, so suspend any debate or rebuttal. Encourage your spouse to give more than one-word or one-sentence answers. You want Picassos here, not just stick-figure drawings! In other words, get full, complete answers to your questions—answers that reveal the full meaning and context of your partner's world.

Try this one night and watch the magic happen.

# 48: DON'T TAKE THE BAIT

MOST EVERYONE WHO has spent any time on a computer has fallen prey to clickbait. It's that picture, headline, or outlandish claim that flashes on our screen. It's strategically placed adjacent to the online article you are reading, and it grabs your attention and makes you wonder, "Could that be true?" Once you click on it, you are usually taken somewhere else—more often than not, a place that has nothing to do with where you started. Sometimes it's just the first step or "click" of many, and minutes or sometimes hours go by before you realize you're nowhere near where you started.

And so it is in our relationship with our spouse. Life seems to be going swimmingly, and then out of the blue that little piece of bait appears in front of you. Maybe it comes in the form of teasing, an exaggerated or obviously unfounded claim about you. It may be just a small irritant that rubs you the wrong way in the moment. Will you take the bait and get hooked?

A few months back, my wife and I were both working out in our home gym (the other half of my office). She finished up and left to start working on her business to-do list. I had a few more sets to do, and I kept going with my headphones on and my music jamming. Kim came back to my office, sat down at my desk, looked at me, and posed a question. I removed my earbuds and asked her to repeat the question, which I quickly answered, and then I returned to my workout.

After two more work-related questions came my way in quick succession, I found myself getting a little irritated. I was ready to fire back with some incredulous sarcasm that wouldn't have been loving or considerate. Instead, I sidestepped the bait and, as calmly and lovingly as I could, posed the following question: "Sweetheart, do you think it would be all right if I finished my workout and then we got together in a few minutes to go over what you'd like to discuss?"

She briefly looked at me, thought a moment, and responded, "Sure. Come get me when you're done." Skirmishing avoided.

When it seems like the bullets might start zinging overhead and you feel you may be wading into hostile territory, don't allow yourself to take the situation personally. Don't pour gasoline onto those already-glowing embers. Instead, choose not to be flanked by what may seem to be a personal or impersonal offensive. You'll never be trapped if you refuse to engage.

In the second agreement of his book *The Four Agreements*, don Miguel Ruiz deftly describes how we should never take anything personally.[25] He goes on to explain that no matter what anyone may say or try to do, when we are tempted to take something personally, we can realize that it is the other person's issue and not ours.

If there are habitual, negative patterns in your relationship, you can have a loving conversation about them. Communicate in a non-confrontational way, and speak from the first-person "I," not a condemning "you." If the practice of not taking things personally and avoiding the tempting bait in your relationship is not already a well-worn routine, when will you start this practice? How can you avoid the pitfalls of becoming ensnared and instead take the time you both need for quality communication with the right timing so it will be received in the best way?

## CHRIS'S TAKE

In Matthew's story, we see the basic principle of *turning toward*. Remember, when we take the time to engage our spouse, as opposed to being silent or belligerent, we are building *trustworthiness*. It's the very small moments of life that make all the difference.

A close friend wrote a book where he discusses a principle called "taking the train."[26] The idea is exactly what we see in Matthew's story. Your spouse comes to you while you're busy. In your mind, you're thinking, "Doesn't she see I don't have time for this?" You typically become irritated, and she knows it. Then the fireworks begin because she feels turned away from. When we "take the train," we choose to pause and think about it for a little bit. We are not required to give an immediate response, so we are taking a detour to ensure we are responding based on our values, not our emotions in the moment. However, every train returns to the station, so be prepared to come back to your spouse with an answer after you have paused and peacefully reviewed the situation. We are gracefully giving ourselves permission to buy some time to return to the conversation without launching into World War III.

My wife will frequently walk in while I'm showering in the morning. In the old days, she would rattle off what seemed to be five hundred questions, and she was looking for answers right then and there. My thoughts were focused on what was in front of me for the day. I would get irritated, and the day would be off to a bad start. After learning the "take the train" concept, my wife still walks in, but now she leaves a list on the counter and simply says, "Take the train." It makes all the difference in the world. I don't feel pressured. I don't feel she is nagging, and I don't feel irritated. I know I have to respond, but I don't have to do it right then and there. I have time to finish getting ready and then address the list on my own time. Sounds simple, but believe me, it changes everything.

Here's a way you can incorporate this into your relationship. Sit with your wife in a quiet place and at a time when you have no encumbrances. Explain that you want to engage her on any and all topics, because you know that's important to her and it's equally important to you. Explain the idea of "taking the train" and talk about how you each can employ it in your communication with each other. Sit back and watch her eyes light up.

# 49: MIND THE GAP

IN HIS FOREWORD to *Prisoners of Our Thoughts*, Stephen Covey summarizes the wisdom of Viktor Frankl: "Between stimulus and response, there is a space. In that space lies our freedom and our power to choose our response. In our response lies our growth and our happiness."[27] I love this quote because it reminds us that we have the power to choose our response in any situation. We are not victims of circumstance. Instead, we can be masters of our circumstance when we choose to respond based on our own core principles and beliefs.

If you walk into the London Underground (commonly known as "the tube"), you will frequently see signs saying "Mind the gap." Their purpose is to make you aware of that dangerous space that lies between the edge of the platform and the tracks. Even though there are yellow and red lines, cautionary warning signs, and recurring audio notifications of the arrival of the next train, people still unwittingly get too close to this danger zone and crane their heads down the track looking and listening for the train. YouTube is full of videos of babies in strollers, children, and many normal-looking adults being rescued from certain death after falling onto the tracks. Although most of these occurrences are unintentional, they still happen in spite of common knowledge and significant, repeated efforts to warn people of potential impending danger.

The scene is not so different in our relationship with our spouse. We receive many subtle and significant signs—some in writing, some via body language; some are even audible cues. Yet we ignore even the most obvious warnings and barrel through the heart and feelings of our bride, claiming ignorance, self-justification, or maybe even just blindness to what is openly visible or lying just under the surface. We act like that bull in the china shop and destroy feelings, emotions, and ideas our wife holds dear.

One of my favorite books is Viktor Frankl's classic, *Man's Search for Meaning*. It is the harrowing, true story of a German psychiatrist whose entire family was murdered in a concentration camp in World War II. Among his immediate family, he was the only survivor. In his book, he reflected that the Nazi guards could take everything else from him, but they couldn't take his ability to think and control his response. He was not in control of his circumstance, but he was in control of his response to it and thus was able to experience his own personal freedom.

I am now a faithful student of "living in the pause," and while I'm not an expert, I am getting stronger every day. When my wife says or does something that could elicit a negative reaction, I pause. I think about who she truly is, who I am, and how I can respond based on my values instead of reacting in the moment. I can respond lovingly, without guile; I can be guided by nobler qualities than that low desire to fire back and injure someone I care for.

How can you start "living in the pause" with your spouse and working to eliminate those unfortunate and often unintended hurtful reactions in your relationship? Sometimes, it's as basic as just asking to take five and circling back to the issue when cooler heads can prevail. Make your own plan to adopt the habit of "living in the pause." This concept works in every area of our lives, and it will help lead you to a greater sense of mastery in your own journey. After thirty days of practice, you'll have a powerful new habit in your toolkit!

## CHRIS'S TAKE

Matthew's story about stimulus and response is important in a variety of ways, but the most essential elements are emotional regulation, self-soothing, and triggers. Minding the gap matters because having some space between stimulus and response is critical for healthy relationships.

Minding the gap deals with what we call *emotional regulation*. The ability to regulate emotion is central in any relationship. If we can't behave and respond in an emotionally mature manner, the relationship will fail. No one will stick around when they feel emotionally abused. It's important to know that in less-than-favorable moments with our spouse, once our heart rate reaches ninety-five beats per minute or above, our frontal lobe essentially shuts down. Why is that important? Well, the frontal lobe is where all logic and reason reside. When it goes offline, complete mayhem breaks out; things are said and done that can damage a relationship permanently.

The greats of relationships are well versed in self-awareness and self-regulation. The idea is that they recognize their own *triggers* and emotions, and when they feel themselves heating up, they take thirty minutes to *self-soothe.*

Here is a practical step you can take to mind the gap and regulate your emotions. The next time you feel things heating up, say to your spouse, "I need thirty minutes," and then go read a magazine. After your time away, ask yourself why you started to get heated. Dig deep and figure it out. It's generally not about what was happening in the moment. Typically, it will be linked to a trigger from times past. Come back and discuss the trigger, where it comes from, and what you need in the future in similar situations.

This is a straightforward exercise you can do to begin the process of regulating your emotions and creating a healthy and loving relationship with your spouse.

# 50: NO SUBSTITUTIONS

I WON'T LIE to you. After more than twenty years of marriage, it can sometimes be challenging to keep our relationship, our romance, and our time together new and exciting. It is easy to fall into old habits. We may get lazy about being present and investing mental and physical energy into intimate time together that is both meaningful and satisfying for each of us.

Leaning on something, or someone, outside the bonds of marriage for satisfaction and fulfillment is a dangerous and destructive habit, one that is always harmful. There is quite a strong pull on most men and boys to look for satisfaction among the always-available, easy-to-find, freely consumable, seemingly anonymous sources of sexual material on the internet. Pornography is pernicious, invasive, and harmful to everyone who is involved with its dangerous allure.

Much of society has become numb to the damaging impact of pornography. Many even feel that the consumption of pornography is not that big a deal. I have to admit that in the past, when the internet became a more integral part of our lives, I did explore and seek out what was available online. I was honestly disgusted with so much of the content, because it was brutally raw and repulsive. The spam I received after visiting some of the sites was just as negative and demoralizing. I knew I had to be free of the downward pull of this material.

I made a promise to myself, my wife, and God that there would be "no substitutions" for intimacy and satisfaction in my marriage. I realized that it was not just about the sex and physical satisfaction but also about preserving the intimacy and implicit trust that I had to have in my relationship with my wife. I knew that if I looked to anything or anyone outside my most valued relationship, I would weaken the bonds of trust and true satisfaction that I had worked so hard to build. I also knew that if I wanted my three children to have a solid example of what a strong, intimate, loving relationship looked like, I had to model it in my own life.

Too many people get trapped in leaning on something or someone outside the bounds of their marriage for satisfaction and fulfillment. Those fleeting, initially attractive distractions—whether they be pornography, another relationship, alcohol, drugs, or something else—have the power to demoralize and destroy. It's also worth noting that they are not enduring.

There is an old Lao Tzu saying, "He who conquers others is strong. He who conquers himself is mighty." I have learned and am continuing to learn how to strengthen my self-regulation and make sure I am being guided by the principles and values that are at the core of my character. My wife and I have so much good in our relationship, and I am grateful that we have been able to continue to build it to last. Through a Christian counselor, reading, watching informative videos, and a lot of prayer, we continue to learn what we both can do to strengthen our love for each other and our commitment to our relationship. We have learned the critical importance of "US," as opposed to "I." I continue to learn more and better ways to help make my wife feel secure in our relationship and my commitment to her, so there are no cracks where doubt and mistrust might try to creep in.

If you commit to keep the emotional, mental, and physical elements of your relationship wrapped together and leading back to no one else besides your spouse, you will succeed in strengthening and celebrating that one unique and enduring bond so it will stand against any illegitimate substitution. If you are truly unhappy and unfulfilled in your current relationship, then fix it or hit eject. Don't drag your family and the institution of marriage through the mud because you are too lazy to own the right solution.

What can you do right now to eliminate any substitutions that you might be making in your relationship? It should not be a solo journey. Talk to your spouse and include her in your growth and healing process. Get help and guidance from those best equipped to support you by surrendering that misplaced personal responsibility and false sense of control. You can begin that renewing journey today.

## CHRIS'S TAKE

As a therapist, I speak with my clients about pornography on a daily basis. Many believe the issue pertains only to men, but believe me, pornography has overcome women as well. It is a substitute for natural relationship, by which we mean relationships with God, self, and others. Engaging with pornography by definition becomes an addictive process. If you have ever been to a twelve-step meeting, you will quickly realize that the steps are built around helping people attach back to God, self, and others. When we are caught in addictive processes, whatever the addiction might be, it becomes our primary love and trust relationship. This is a betrayal of our spouse. Our spouse should be our primary love and trust relationship. No substitutes.

I had the opportunity to film the renowned expert Patrick Carnes for an online course for therapists. Patrick leads the world in sexual addiction treatment, and you know his clients' names all too well. During our time together, he discussed with me the reality of the overwhelming destruction sexual addiction wreaks within relationships. He explained the inevitable loss of everything people hold dear: wife, children, job, and friends. We talked about the fact that pornography is not real. It creates a false picture of sexuality, and in turn a false picture of intimacy.

Your wife will never behave that way. She's your wife, the mother of your children, and the daughter of your in-laws. She holds a position that by definition deserves respect, and acting out what you've seen on the screen is not respect. I also don't have to tell you that on your best day, you will never perform like the men you see on the screen. It's not real.

Every day, we hear of sexual trafficking. The mere thought of it is disgusting, and I'm sure raises the hair on the back of your neck. Well, know this: the porn industry is deeply tied in to sex trafficking. So every time you watch it, you are contributing to a plague that is vile beyond words.

We live in a world that travels at the speed of light, and it's important we find time to detach from it and relax. Substituting fake intimacy for the real thing will damage you. Know that, and adjust.

Here are a few ways you can accomplish this. Porn-proof your environment. Have your spouse download porn blockers on your phone and computer. Let her control the passwords, and have all reports and alerts sent directly to her. Don't travel by tempting places. If you know there's a porn shop on Main Street, drive down another street. At the mall, avoid Victoria's Secret. The images there can tempt you. Live by the acronym *HALT*, which stands for hungry, angry, lonely, and tired. When you feel any of these, get them taken care of. This is a simple tool that can be very effective in eliminating the emotional vulnerability to compulsive behavior.

By taking these simple steps, you will be protecting yourself and attaching back to natural relationships. Most importantly, you will build trust with your wife.

# 51: COMFORTABLE WITH DISCOMFORT

THERE IS NO doubt that we live in a world which seems to be striving more and more to escape from the minor aches and pains of daily living. Whether it's physical, mental, or emotional discomfort, it seems that all of our devices are full of ads describing recently discovered diseases and forms of pain. There's always a drug, a product, or some alterative that claims to relieve that pain! Imagine the size of the pantry you'd need if you wanted to take every food, drug, vitamin, or supplement that is touted as a solution to one condition or another.

It is not easy, or preferable, to exist in a state of discomfort. Our basic human inclination is to run from pain and pursue pleasure. But if we are willing to endure a little bit of heat, we can refine that raw, ugly, impure piece of metal into pure, beautiful gold. We may revel in success and enjoy celebration and achievement for a time, but it always seems to be the trials where we are called to dig deeper and learn life's grander lessons.

I'm really speaking about commitment. Whether you're on the mountaintop of your relationship, with a grand view of beauty and success, or in that dark valley where it seems pretty dire and you're not sure if you're going to make it back into the sunshine, commitment is what matters. If you and your spouse have truly committed to each other, then it's not a question of "if," it's a question of "how."

Hindsight is 20/20. It is easy to look in the rearview mirror and watch something get smaller as you speed forward. It is much more difficult to have it take up your entire windshield. I have to admit I don't take pleasure in my own foibles or in the messier experiences of life. In the moment, what's happening may look inescapable, but that doesn't mean it is. I am learning that life is full of seasons, and none of them goes on forever.

Like all couples, Kim and I have repeatedly experienced challenges, and they have come in three different forms. There have been distinct personal issues she has faced, distinct personal issues I have faced, and distinct issues that the two of us have faced. Whatever the type of issue, I think a growth mindset is the key to learning how to "play through" the dark valleys of our lives. In every chapter of this book, there are ideas, practices, concepts, and suggestions that—when taken as an entire framework or system— will help you build a stronger and more enduring relationship that better equips you for life. Your partner is just that: your *partner*. When you and your spouse are agents of support for one another, you will have more confidence, more strength, and a greater ability to work through times of discomfort.

Several years ago, my wife was plagued by the inability to breathe freely and fully. We talked about it, prayed, and went to a slew of doctors trying to find what we could possibly do for her so she would find some relief and freedom. The suffering seemed unfair to her, and it certainly had negative effects on our relationship as well. Yet we continued to be dedicated on all fronts. I strived to be her biggest cheerleader, confidant, and partner in battle. We eventually worked through it, and she was able to conquer that challenge; she is now free from any of the old breathing problems. My wife, too, has been there for me in those dark-valley experiences with the assurance that "I'm not going anywhere. I'm here for you, and we'll get through it together."

There are countless examples of strain, stress, and discomfort in our world that all lead to growth, increased resilience, and beauty. None of these opportunities are destinations; they're just brief stops along the track. By getting comfortable with a little discomfort and seeing the bench strength of "US," you will be able to emerge from the trials with your spouse, both of you ready to enjoy that beautiful summit view.

How can you work to right your perspective of discomfort in your relationship and embrace those opportunities to stretch and grow, with your wife as your dedicated life partner?

## CHRIS'S TAKE

Many things are transpiring in Matthew's story. Two that deserve our attention are *commitment* and *trust*. Here's why they are important.

By commitment, we mean we are fully emotionally invested in the relationship, come what may. We think, "This is my journey for life." We are *not* thinking, "Feels good now, but if it gets painful, I have options." Until we arrive at "This is my journey, till death do us part," our marriage hasn't even started. Why not? Because if we haven't decided we're all in, there is a plan B, and if there is a plan B, plan A won't work. Having a plan B is a very common approach to life, and it's problematic because it creates conditional commitment in relationships.

Pain will always pursue pleasure, meaning relief of the pain, but that desire for relief doesn't mean we have to leave our relationships. We can take the time to mature emotionally. We can face whatever problems come our way relationally, stretch ourselves, and find a safe harbor. It's not easy, but it will grow you and mature you emotionally. Every one of those difficult moments provides the opportunity for transformation.

All too often, we are masters at snatching defeat out of the jaws of victory. Why do we do that? The answer is fairly simple. We have trained our brain to check out when the going gets tough. Truth be told, your brain is designed to keep you safe, so it *tells* you to check out. However, if we are going to have successful relationships, careers, and friendships, we are going to have to do things that are uncomfortable and scary at times. If we recognize that and push through, we create new neural set points in the brain—set points that are set to victory and not defeat.

If you take the time to push through, you will also be adding to the basis of *trustworthiness* in your relationship. How? Simple. As time goes by, your spouse will develop a heartfelt sense that you are there for the long run. You have their back.

Here is a simple thing you can do to reset. The next time a challenge in your relationship comes ashore, recognize it for what it is: a moment in time. The sky hasn't fallen; the apocalypse hasn't begun. That simple reminder will interrupt the potentially defeating thought processes and begin to create new neural set points that default to solutions, not defeat.

# 52: GARBAGE IN, GARBAGE OUT

THERE'S AN OLD programmer's saying, "Garbage in, garbage out." It really can apply to all areas of our lives, whether it's what we eat, what we watch or listen to, what we read, or even those self-defeating thoughts we allow to become permanent furniture in the rooms of our mind. Quality consumption, in all of its forms, is critical to our sustained happiness and success.

Anatoly Karpov is a Russian chess grandmaster and a former world chess champion. One of his widely touted champion's sayings is "To be champion requires more than simply being a strong player; one has to be a strong human being as well." There it is again. Physical, emotional, spiritual, and mental toughness all contribute to help us win the day.

You have a choice about what form of fuel you run on in each area of your life, and they all have a direct impact on what kind of husband, friend, and partner you are going to be. Poor, cheap, and ineffective choices may seem easy in the short term, but they can result in disastrous consequences over time. Sustainability and consistency breed lasting success. It's not a diet; it's a lifestyle choice. If those choices are informed by your deeply held values and life principles, you have really struck gold. You will find yourself happy, at peace, and fulfilled.

Success in a relationship is not only about making good personal decisions. It is about coming together and making those healthy decisions as a couple, giving your relationship the care and feeding it needs to remain vital. Both you and your spouse have both personal and relationship responsibilities. Failure in either area will result in damage to the relationship. The biggest challenge is that you can't just make what you think are the best decisions for your spouse!

I have always been a person who enjoys physical activity. I love engaging in active outdoor ventures. I enjoy challenging myself to the point that I am physically spent and sore, so I feel I have *done* something. For me, this desire is intrinsic; it does not depend on influence from somewhere or someone else.

My wife also values activity and exercise, and, for a time, it worked well for her when she had someone to help keep her accountable and focused, whether it was a trainer or a workout partner. But when she felt under pressure from work or family responsibilities, her exercise and self-care was the first thing to go. It would often cascade into increased stress levels, physical discomfort, and frustration for her, and sometimes into a sense of resentment toward me, since I always seemed to have time to exercise. My underlying concern was her well-being; it didn't seem healthy that she was almost always willing to put the needs of others above herself. Many consider this a noble quality, and in the correct perspective it is. But taken to the extreme, it is unhealthy and not sustainable.

Through prayer, education, and reading, and through our shared approach of renewing our personal relationship and commitment to each other, I have learned how to broach this and other sensitive issues through a more loving and genuine discourse. Modeling self-care in my own behavior and gently supporting and encouraging her health and wellness in my mental, verbal, and physical interactions with her has continued to strengthen our bond in many ways.

This is not a "Fake it till you make it" scenario. It is really all about making the active, conscious decision to invest in, feed, and nurture yourself with the highest-quality food in each area of your life.

Take an inventory of what you have stockpiled and what you're ingesting today. Are you fully equipped to thrive in those personal and relationship struggles? Can you commit to trashing those old, stale, nutritionally empty habits and activities that are failing to strengthen you and your number-one human relationship?

## CHRIS'S TAKE

The most important aspect of life is being a guardian of our thoughts. Our thought life sets the stage—spiritually, physically, and emotionally—for how we react, respond, and engage in all of life. In Matthew's story, we see two significant topics being addressed: *commitment* and *the Four Horsemen of the Apocalypse*. Here's why each are important.

Commitment, as we have discussed, means we are fully emotionally "in" the relationship—all aspects of it. There is a decision made within our hearts and minds that we will do whatever it takes to make the relationship last, and we will not waver from that path. That takes extreme discipline—discipline that escapes most of us in various areas of our lives but that cannot be absent in the fundamentals of our relationship.

If we don't exercise the muscle of our relationship daily, it will weaken and fail. One of the ways we can strengthen our relationship is by eliminating the Four Horsemen of the Apocalypse. Matthew explained that his desire was for his wife's health. However, there were probably moments when that concern might have felt to Kim like criticism or contempt, and those are predictors of divorce. By replacing criticism with a soft startup and contempt with a culture of appreciation, we are showing commitment to the relationship. We are eradicating the malignancies that so often plague relationships.

Success in all things requires a deep intentional commitment to processes that are geared toward effective outcomes. Throughout this book, we have covered cutting-edge research by some of the greatest in the field of marriage and family therapy. The book you are holding in your hands is your yellow brick road. All you have to do is follow it.

You don't have to tackle everything in one day. Instead, slowly, steadily, and methodically, you can begin building each floor of a sound relationship house. None of the principles is beyond you, but they do require you to be intentional and committed to the process. Remember, this is a marathon, not a sprint. Small, intentional steps in the physical, emotional, and spiritual areas of your life will immediately begin to pay dividends, both to you and to the woman you have chosen to spend your life with.

# GLOSSARY

This glossary focuses on John Gottman's components of the sound relationship house as explained in *The Seven Principles for Making Marriage Work* (2015). It also includes some other key relationship concepts. We encourage you to notice how these things show up in your own relationship.

**Accepting influence.** Elevating our spouse's opinions and thoughts to the same level as our own.

**Bids.** Acts of gesturing to get someone's attention—for example, by asking "How was your day?" These small interactions create the doorway to trustworthiness. They are a prime example of turning toward.

**Commitment.** If trust is something you feel, commitment is something you do. It's taking your partner with you wherever you go. Commitment is not governed by some kind of obligation or legal contract. It's governed by a sense of partnership on the journey.

**Contempt.** Mockery, sarcasm, and hostile humor with the intent to make one's partner feel stupid, foolish, or otherwise inferior.

**Couple payoff.** This is a game theory concept. The idea is that the couple maximizes their payoff for any given interaction. For example, faced with three choices—the husband cleaning the house by himself, the couple cleaning the house together, or the wife cleaning the house by herself—the couple would choose the approach that achieves the maximum payoff for both.

**Creating shared meaning.** A couple develops a mutual view of the world around them. This view is developed by creating rituals.

**Criticism.** A complaint taken to the next level by including statements that are blaming, attack character, or are otherwise insulting.

**Deep understanding.** Moving beyond hearing to a felt sense of mutual experience or empathy.

**Defensiveness.** Defending oneself from real or perceived criticism by making excuses, deflecting blame, or otherwise avoiding responsibility.

**Emotional regulation.** A person's ability to effectively manage and respond to an emotional experience.

**Eternal woo.** The undying commitment and dedication to continuously looking for ways to court your partner.

**Friendship system.** A foundation for commitment and trust, consisting of love mapping, sharing fondness and admiration, and turning toward.

**Game theory.** Originally, game theory was created by mathematicians to help predict economic outcomes. Later, psychologists used it to examine outcomes of human behavior. We can utilize game theory to predict the outcome of a couple's interaction. When two people interact in a given way, game theory helps us determine whether the interaction will benefit one person, the other, or both.

**HALT.** This stands for the trip wires that can lead to addictive behaviors: hungry, angry, lonely, and tired. If you are hungry, eat. If you are tired, rest. If you are lonely, reach out. If you are tired, rest.

**Intentional listening.** The act of listening beyond the words that are being spoken. It is a deep heartfelt quest into empathy, where we not only understand what has been spoken, we feel it.

**Life dreams.** All couples dream of what their life should be together: number of children, age of retirement, where to live, and so on. There are also life dreams at an individual level: what we could accomplish in our careers, our communities, and our personal lives. Great couples get to know those individual life dreams and help one another achieve them.

**Love mapping.** An in-depth knowledge of your spouse's internal world achieved through asking open-ended questions on all matters of life.

**Making life dreams come true.** Knowing our spouse's dreams in life and actively helping them achieve those dreams.

**Mindfulness.** The ability to be in the present and not preoccupied with the past or the future.

**Negative perspective.** A critical, pessimistic outlook that develops when the couple's friendship system is breaking down.

**Negative sentiment override.** This is a result of living in a negative perspective without intervention. When more than half of a couple's interactions are negative, a complete rewriting of history begins, such that nothing good can be remembered in the relationship.[28]

**Perpetual problems.** Issues that will be part of the relationship as long as it lasts. Sixty-nine percent of couples' problems are perpetual. The ability to deal with these will depend on the couple's ability to create good conversation with good emotion around things they will never agree on.

**Physical touch.** A key component of relationships because of its positive physical and psychological benefits. Physical benefits range from enhanced immune system to cardiac function. Psychological benefits range in scope from affirmation to acceptance.

**Positive comps.** Positive thoughts about each other and the marriage are so pervasive that they tend to supersede the couple's negative feelings.

**Positive perspective.** The result of a strong friendship system. The relationship feels good to the couple.

**Positive sentiment.** The couple's thoughts and memories of the relationship are good. They remember all the good times and focus on those. They don't hold bad memories at the forefront of their minds.

**Rituals of connection.** Relationship-strengthening rites, practices, or observations that the couple creates together. An example would be always saying "Hi, Sweetie" when entering each other's presence.

**Secure attachment.** A deep sense that your partner is always there for you. Securely attached couples are comfortable being dependent on one another as well as being independent.

**Self-soothing.** The process of reducing an overexcited emotional system via deep breathing, reading, or other techniques. Example: conflict begins to escalate, and a couple separates for thirty minutes to read a magazine.

**Shared meaning system.** A mutual understanding created through the use of rituals, roles, goals, and symbols. When you get married, you create something that has never existed before. A shared meaning system should exist for every couple, no matter how much you and your partner have in common, no matter how long you've been together.

**Sharing fondness and admiration.** The ability and determination to look for the good qualities and characteristics of your spouse, focus on them, and speak about them.

**Solvable problems.** These are problems that have concrete answers. For example, you forgot to take the trash out. That can be solved by taking the trash out in the future.

**Stonewalling.** Actively disengaging from a conversation. Includes looking away and not responding to questions. Often occurs when one partner is feeling overwhelmed by the conversation.

**Subjective reality.** This concept deals with the idea that in any interaction involving a couple, or any combination of people, there are multiple interpretations of what is happening or has happened, and they are all real. For instance, when a couple has an argument, they each remember it in very specific and different ways.

**The Four Horsemen of the Apocalypse.** Criticism, defensiveness, contempt, and stonewalling. When present within a couple's arguments, they predict divorce with 94 percent accuracy.[29]

**Trigger.** An interaction or event in which the emotions of one or both partners become heightened in a positive or negative way.

**Trustworthiness.** The knowledge that your spouse is there for you, achieved by continually turning toward your spouse and being present in the small things of life—for example, by putting your phone down when your spouse is speaking to you as opposed to ignoring them. Trustworthiness takes sustained effort and is achieved over a fifteen- to twenty-five-year period.

**Turning against.** Responding to your spouse in a way that is hostile. This will erode trustworthiness in the relationship.

**Turning away.** Not responding when your spouse tries to engage you. This too erodes trustworthiness.

**Turning toward.** Actively engaging your spouse when they engage you. An example would be looking up from your computer when your spouse is speaking to you, stopping typing, and participating fully in a conversation. This will build trustworthiness in a relationship.

**Understanding.** A heartfelt sense of our spouse's positions or beliefs on all matters of life and death. This goes beyond merely the facts we take in.

**US.** The relationship itself. It is the essence of the couple. In any relationship, you have one individual, you have another individual, and you have "US."

# RESOURCES

## BOOKS

Chapman, Gary. 2015. *The Five Love Languages.* Chicago: Northfield Publishing.

Ford, Debbie. 2004. *The Right Questions: Ten Essential Questions to Guide You to an Extraordinary Life.* New York: HarperOne.

Gottman, John, and Nan Silver. 2015. *The Seven Principles for Making Marriage Work.* New York: Harmony Books.

Gottman, John, with Nan Silver. 2007. *Why Marriages Succeed or Fail.* New York: Bloomsbury.

van der Kolk, Bessel. 2015. *The Body Keeps the Score.* New York: Penguin.

## VIDEOS

RelateWell video series by Richard Marks: https://relatewellinstitute.com/core

Gott Sex video series by the Gottman institute: www.Gottsex.com

# NOTES

1    Gottman, J., and N. Silver. 2015. *The Seven Principles for Making Marriage Work*. New York: Harmony Books.

2    Gottman, J. 2011. *The Science of Trust*. New York: W. W. Norton & Company.

3    Gottman, J. 2013. "Summer Romance: Turning Towards." Podcast audio, July 19. *The Gottman Relationship Blog.* https://gottman3.rssing.com/chan-11308500/all_p4.html.

4    Aron, A., E. Melinat, E. Aron, R. Vallone, and R. Bator. 1997. "The experimental generation of interpersonal closeness: A procedure and some preliminary findings." *Personality and Social Psychology* 23 (4): 363–77. doi:10.1177/0146167297234003.

5    Chapman, G. 2015. *The Five Love Languages*. Chicago: Northfield Publishing.

6    Gray, J. 2012. *Men Are from Mars, Women Are from Venus*. New York: Harper.

7    Patterson-Neubert, A. 2004. "Purdue study shows men, women share same planet." *Purdue News*. February 17. https://www.purdue.edu/uns/html4ever/2004/040217. MacGeorge.sexroles.html.

8   Haviland-Jones, J., H. Rosario, P. Wilson, and T. McGuire. 2005. "An environmental approach to positive emotion: Flowers." *Evolutionary Psychology* 3 (1). doi:10.1177/147470490500300109.

9   Ferriss, T. 2011. *The 4-Hour Work Week.* London: Ebury Press.

10  Lisitsa, E. 2014. "The Trouble with Contempt." *The Gottman Institute.* March 5. https://www.gottman.com/blog/self-care-contempt/.

11  Kouros, C. D., C. E. Merrilees, and E. M. Cummings. 2008. "Marital conflict and children's emotional security in the context of parental depression." *Journal of Marriage and the Family,* 70 (3), 684–697. https://doi.org/10.1111/j.1741-3737.2008.00514.x

12  Kelly, J. 2017. "'Shocking' new research finds friendships are key to good health." *UVA Today.* May 26. https://news.virginia.edu/content/shocking-new-research-finds-friendships-are-key-good-health.

13  Gottman, J., and N. Silver. 2015. *The Seven Principles for Making Marriage Work.* New York: Harmony Books.

14  Emoto, M. 2005. *The Hidden Messages in Water.* New York: Atria.

15  Brittle, Z. 2015. "Manage Conflict: Accepting Influence." *The Gottman Institute.* April 29. https://www.gottman.com/blog/manage-conflict-accepting-influence/.

16  Kelly, J. 2017. "'Shocking' new research finds friendships are key to good health." *UVA Today*. May 26. https://news. virginia.edu/content/shocking-new-research-finds-friendships-are-key-good-health.

17  Hanson, R. 2012. "See the Good in Others." *Psychology Today*. May 12. https://www.psychologytoday.com/us/blog/your-wise-brain/201205/see-the-good-in-others.

18  Gottman, J., and N. Silver. 2015. *The Seven Principles for Making Marriage Work*. New York: Harmony Books.

19  Ford, D. 2004. *The Right Questions: Ten Essential Questions to Guide You to an Extraordinary Life*. New York: HarperOne.

20  Patterson-Neubert, A. 2004. "Purdue study shows men, women share same planet." *Purdue News*. February 17. https://www.purdue.edu/uns/html4ever/2004/040217. MacGeorge.sexroles.html.

21  Dolan, E. 2019. "Couples Who Communicate More About Sex Have Better Sex, Study Finds." *PsyPost*. June 21. https://www.psypost.org/2019/06/couples-who-communicate-more-about-sex-tend-to-have-better-sex-study-finds-53916.

22  Allen, S. 2018. *The Science of Gratitude*. Berkeley, CA: Greater Good Science Center.

23  Gottman, J., with N. Silver. 2007. *Why Marriages Succeed or Fail*. New York: Bloomsbury.

24  Beckwith, M. 2009. "The Discovery of Eternal Truth."
    Interview by Tami Simon. Podcast audio, June 30. *Insights at the Edge.* https://resources.soundstrue.com/transcript/michael-beckwith-the-discovery-of-eternal-truth/.

25  Ruiz, M. 2018. *The Four Agreements.* San Rafael, CA: Amber-Allen Publishing.

26  Clarke, D. 2019. *Men Are Clams, Women Are Crowbars.* Carol Stream, IL: Tyndale Publishing.

27  Pattakos, A. 2010. *Prisoners of Our Thoughts.* Oakland, CA: Berrett-Koehler.

28  Hawkins, M. W., S. Carrère, and J. M. Gottman. 2004. "Marital sentiment override: Does it influence couples' perceptions?" *Journal of Marriage and Family* 64 (1): 193–201. doi.org/10.1111/j.1741-3737.2002.00193.x

29  Buehlman, K. T., J. M. Gottman, and L. F. Katz. 1992. "How a couple views their past predicts their future: Predicting divorce from an oral history interview." *Journal of Family Psychology* 5 (3–4): 295–318. doi:10.1037/0893-3200.5.3-4.295.

# CONNECT WITH THE AUTHORS

📷 Instagram
@KickassCouplesNation

📘 Facebook
@Kickasscouplesnation

💼 LinkedIn
@Kickasscouplesnation

▶️ YouTube
@KickAss Couples Podcast

🎵 TikTok
@Kickasscouplesnation

**matthewphoffman.com**

## MATTHEW HOFFMAN

MATTHEW HOFFMAN is a kickass husband and successful business-man, coach, father, and son. Matthew is an expert at leading men to become the most powerful and effective husbands they can be. He founded the *Kickass Couples* podcast, where he interviews successful couples across varied backgrounds, life stages, and professions. He shares their stories of how they established their relationships, navigated challenges, and created a union built to weather the storms of life. Matthew believes every successful marriage rests on a foundation of commitment, communication, and determination to resolve the solvable conflicts that arise.

## CHRIS CAMBAS

CHRIS CAMBAS is a licensed marriage and family therapist certified in Gottman Method Couples Therapy. Chris operates out of a deep desire to help others claim victory and healing in their number-one relationship. For over twenty years, he has helped couples and individuals overcome the obstacles that stand in the way of their happiness and success. Chris has also worked with thousands of therapists, strengthening their practices through ongoing education and training to prepare them to excel in their practices with people just like you.